The Produce Chef

The Produce Chef

Matt Clark

Cooking with native and wild ingredients

NEW HOLLAND

First published in Australia in 2009 by
New Holland Publishers (Australia) Pty Ltd
Sydney • Auckland • London • Cape Town

1/66 Gibbes Street Chatswood NSW 2067 Australia
218 Lake Road Northcote Auckland New Zealand
86 Edgware Road London W2 2EA United Kingdom
80 McKenzie Street Cape Town 8001 South Africa

National Library of Australia Cataloguing-in-Publication entry

Clark, Matt.

The produce chef : cooking with native and wild ingredients
/ Matt Clark.

ISBN: 9781741108347

Notes: Includes index.

Subjects: Cookery, Australian.
           Cookery--Australia.
           Wild foods--Australia.
           Recipes--Australia.

           641.5994

Publisher: Linda Williams
Publishing Manager: Lliane Clarke
Editor and proofreader: Kay Proos
Designer: Tania Gomes
Photographs: Matt Clark, istock and Graeme Gillies/NHIL pp22-23, 77, 82-83,
100-101, 114-115, 128-129, 144-145
Production Manager: Olga Dementiev
Printer: SNP/Leefung Printing Co. Ltd (China)

10 9 8 7 6 5 4 3 2 1

Contents

About the author

Matt Clark grew up in a small coastal town in Tasmania where there was a huge emphasis on cooking fresh, local produce with an abundant supply of products at hand. This is where his passion for fresh food was born along with his interest in fine cuisine, taking him all over the continent in search of new and interesting ideas and products. Since then, he has travelled the world and worked Australia-wide.

Matt has worked in five-star hotels, resorts, fine-dining restaurants, cafes and pubs, and has developed his own style of cooking that is quite experimental in the way he uses produce and ingredients. He has currently settled in Perth, Western Australia due to the diverse selection of produce and the vast degree of land and cultural awareness.

Matt constantly pushes himself to find different products and styles of cooking and is forever sharing his ideas through radio interviews, magazine and newspaper articles, and by bringing forward a creative menu for all to indulge in.

Contact Matt for product supplies and other cooking hints at:
www.culinarymadness.com

Preface

A lot of people ask 'why?' when they discover the array of foods that I choose to cook with. Well, I think that the answer lies somewhere within the soul of this book. I started getting involved with native Australian produce when I was running a kitchen in an area where these kind of creations were not in practice which inspired me to do something different. I was sick of doing the same thing as everyone else and decided to incorporate some different ingredients into my cooking. I soon discovered that this brought on a lot of interest from consumers with them demanding more and more each week.

What I like about these products is the many flavours and aromas that a lot of people are yet to discover. Australia holds a backyard of amazing flavours that are unlike anything you will find anywhere else and most of us are still missing out. Flavours and textures that you never even dreamed of existing are probably staring at you right outside your lounge room window.

Most recipes contained in this book are not set in stone. The amazing thing about cooking is that you can twist things around and add your own touch. Think of a recipe as a guide to your own creation, it's the method that is important, not necessarily the ingredients. Just make sure to choose ingredients that will work together and you're well on your way to successful cooking. For example, chocolate and coconut go well together as do coconut and chicken but you would not want to mix all three—you get the idea. This book provides you with enough cooking techniques and ideas for you to mix and match your own dishes and create your own signature masterpiece. The only limit is that of your imagination.

Happy creations.

Matt Clark.

Common wild ingredients used in this book

Native plants and herbs

Many of these are found in supermarkets or specialty delis, or by mail order online.

Kakadu Plum

The Kakadu plum is predominately found in the open forest areas of the top end of Australia. It grows on a tall slender tree with rough greyish coloured bark and large light-green leaves. It is a small oval-shaped fruit with a large stone covered in a thin green skin.

The Kakadu plum has been identified worldwide as having the highest content of vitamin C of any fruit, with 3000mg of vitamin C per 100g of fruit. Oranges for example, contain just 50mg of vitamin C per 100g.

The taste of the plum has a fresh citrus taste. It is usually used to make jams and chutneys where it will lose some tartness. Adding sugar will produce a honey-like flavour.

Lemon Aspen

The lemon aspen tree is mostly found in the tropical regions of Australia but it has been known to grow quite successfully in the southern areas as long as the soil is well drained with lots of water.

The tree has dark green, oval shaped leaves and bunches of small yellow flowers that have an attractive strong scent with clusters of the fruit. The fruit is about the size of a small grape and is quite firm with a pale yellow colour. The flavour is an intense tartish lemon that is very strong, but then follows up with an almost honey-like flavour.

A lot of people use this fruit in place of lemons but neglect to realise that there is more to this ingredient than just the citrus taste—any dish will be enhanced with its own unique twist.

You can match lemon aspen well with fish, seafood and chicken. It also goes well in cakes and desserts. The best way to use it is to blitz them up in a food processor with a little water and incorporate this into the recipe. You may need to strain the puree as the seeds can become hard in older varieties. Puree will also work well in a dressing or a marinade.

Bush Tomato

Bush tomatoes, also known as the desert raisin, mountain pepper or Akudjura, grow on small bushes of about 10-20mm in diameter. They have a unique pungent, earthy tomato flavour with a caramel-type background. After ripening, the fruits remain on the plant and dry to resemble a raisin. The fruits are most commonly dried and ground and used as a seasoning for stews, sauces and casseroles. They should be used sparingly as they can be very strong and can quickly overpower other ingredients.

Lemon Myrtle

Lemon myrtle can be found in warm moist climates, particularly along the east coast of Australia. It is becoming quite easy to source. The amazing thing about lemon myrtle is that it has a superb lemon fragrance that comes out more distinctively when it rains.

The most popular part to use is the leaf, which resembles a small bayleaf. The flowers and seeds are also usable. You can buy lemon myrtle in almost any form, depending on what you are using it for, crushed, whole, dried, fresh, or ground. You can also take a big branch and hang it up in your cupboard away from direct sunlight and leave to air dry. Once dried, the leaves will keep in an airtight container for six months. The crushed variety is the most versatile and can be used in marinades and incorporated through various recipes.

Lemon myrtle blends very well with fish and chicken. Sprinkle some on top of the fish and then place into the oven for 10-15 minutes to enjoy a beautiful lemon taste through the fish. You can also toss it through some freshly cooked rice for an amazing aroma. You can even finely slice the fresh leaf and cook in stir-frys or toss through vegetables.

Illawarra Plum

The Illawarra plum is a commonly used ingredient. It is a small plum with a strong plum-like flavour ending with a tartish aftertaste.

The tree will grow in most soil types and can adapt to most climates. It will not overgrow in the backyard and will also grow quite slowly.

Like the riberry, the plum is commonly used to make sauces and works well with game meats such as kangaroo and venison. It also goes well in cakes and muffins and surprisingly fits with seafood, especially shellfish.

The main rule when cooking Illawarra plums is to cook them in a stainless steel saucepan as they will tend to take on the flavour of an aluminium one, making them bitter and unpalatable.

Macadamia Nut

The macadamia nut originated in Australia but back in the late 18th century, the seeds were transported from Australia to Hawaii by early Americans for major plantations. It is an Australian native plant that is in demand worldwide for a variety of uses.

The trees typically grow in coastal subtropical conditions particularly on the New South Wales and Queensland borders of Australia. Macadamia trees have hard green leaves with white flowers and clusters of shelled nuts. The tree itself can grow up to 12 metres in height.

The trees will grow well in the right conditions but develop quite slowly. They need a good water supply and protection from harsh weather conditions, such as heavy winds or frosts. You can grow them from seeds but the best option is to buy an established plant from a nursery. The nut itself is very high in fat and oil content, and is a very high energy source. Most supermarkets stock them in either raw or roasted, whole, crushed or meal forms.

There are endless ways to enjoy this superb nut. They are quite nice just roasted in the oven for 8-10 minutes until golden brown and eaten by themselves.

They also match very well with orange and chocolate. You can crush them slightly and fold them through cakes or muffin mix or even bread dough. You could even try a macadamia nut and caramel tart drizzled with chocolate. They can take the place of nuts such as walnuts or peanuts. They also match well with fish and chicken and provide a great alternative to stuffing mix.

Pepperberries

Pepperberries are a great alternative to cracked black pepper. They have a fairly intense hot pepper/chilli type flavour with an amazing fruity background.

The plant grows in the South East of Australia and both leaves and berries can be used. The berries are fleshy and black and about the size of a pea. They can be used whole or dried. The fresh berries are great in sauces or marinades. giving out an intense burgundy colour, while the leaves are particularly good in marinades, providing a robust hot pepper burst.

Quandong

The quandong, otherwise known as the wild or native peach, is a truly unique native Australian fruit found in the hot and drier regions of the country. Traditionally the quandong was an important food source for Australian Aborigines and was considered a suitable substitute for meat, especially when game meat was in short supply. Ripe red quandong fruits would be eaten raw or dried for later use. They were also used for several important medicinal uses.

The fruits are 2–3 cm in diameter, spherical to pear-shaped, with yellow to bright red skin and a relatively thin white to brown flesh. The flavour has been compared with that of a good red wine. They are commonly used in jams, pies, puddings and sauces. It has been proved that the fruit can be dried and frozen for eight years or more, without losing any flavour at all.

Saltbush

Saltbush is a familiar sight over large areas of the dry inland of Australia. Saltbush grows well in dry arid areas and retains a salty flavour in its leaves. It is a grey-blue shrub that grows up to 3 metres high and can spread to 5 metres wide. It is a long living plant and grows strongly after rain.

It has a fresh salty flavour with a very slight mintish undertone that seems to be balanced with a light sweetness.

Dried saltbush leaves go amazingly well on a roast leg of lamb or with seafood and chicken. Just mix a small amount with some oil and then rub into the meat before cooking. Alternatively, it can be used to season stews or casseroles or even sprinkled on baked potatoes before cooking.

Riberry

Riberries are a unique fruit with a distinct clove-like flavour with hints of cinnamon and nutmeg. They are a part of the Lilly pilly family and are small fruits about the size of a blueberry which range in colour from pale pink to a bright purple. They are often referred to as the clove lilly pilly.

The tree mostly grows up the east coast of Australia and is often seen in parks and gardens, especially throughout Sydney. They have quite diverse growing conditions as long as they have access to plenty of water. They can easily be obtained from any good nursery.

The berry naturally pairs well with apples in cooking—in apple crumble or apple pie or even apple sauce.

While they are usually used to make a sauce or chutney, they are also great in cakes or muffins and ice-creams and sorbets. The berries are also good just to eat on their own.

Rosella

Rosella (*Hibiscus sabdariffa*) is an exotic plant thought to have been introduced to Australia thousands of years ago by Indonesian fishermen. Australians have since adopted it as a native plant creating uses for it in jams, relishes, tea, cocktails and even for medicinal purposes.

It is an amazing plant that most commonly grows in the tropical regions of the country. All parts of this bushy shrub can be eaten, with the leaves being a great substitute for spinach and going well in salads. The roots can be eaten and treated just like parsnip.

The main flower, the calyx, can be eaten raw as a vegetable in salads, or boiled in water. They are commonly sold in jars in a syrup where they can be turned into chutneys or placed straight into a glass of good champagne. They are also great in ice-cream or as a replacement for cranberry sauce for turkey.

The most popular description of the flavour is that of raspberry and rhubarb.

Warrigal Greens

Warrigal greens are one of the first native Australian plants to become popular with European settlers. Captain Cook fed his crew and convicts on these leaves and took some back to England for plantations.

They grow all year round but the quality and quantity are reduced through the cooler months. They are often mistaken for a weed. Their

small arrow-shaped leaves and medium-green colour, with a distinct light spinach flavour, make them more 'meatier' than spinach.

Warrigal greens can be used in place of spinach and go well in a quiche, tossed through a stir-fry or even in a salad. However, caution must be taken because the leaves have a high oxalate concentration. Leaves should be blanched for 1-2 minutes to remove soluble oxalates, then placed into iced water. Despite this, they can be eaten raw in small doses as you need a large amount to cause concern.

Wattleseed

Wattleseed comes from the Wattle or Acacia tree. A national Australian emblem, they are found all over the country. There are hundreds of different species, with many commonly found in our own backyards.

They look like a small shrub and have been in use for centuries, both as a nutritious food source and even for medicinal purposes. Aboriginals have been used these trees for antiseptic lotions for cuts and burns and they also use the timber for making boomerangs. Wattleseed is also very good for you. It has a high nutrient value that is up there with products such as wheat and rice. It is even competing with some meats in protein and energy.

Typically, the wattleseed is used in its dry ground form which is how it is most commonly bought. Depending on the variety, wattleseed will vary in strength and colour but will have a distinctive coffee-like flavour with hints of chocolate and hazelnuts. The lighter the seed, the stronger the choc-nut taste. This obviously makes it great for desserts but it does not stop there. There are many ways we can incorporate this amazing seed into our diet, whether it be sweet or savoury.

Wattleseed is tasty in ice-cream or in bread or muffins. You can use it in a cheesecake or fold it through some whipped cream for cakes or pavlovas. In some cases its best if you put the seeds into a little boiling water to infuse, then add to the recipe. This will enhance the flavour much more and give a greater distribution through the food.

Incorporate this astounding seed into your cooking by substituting it for chocolate or by matching it with some hazelnuts in a tart or pudding. It's even great as a replacement for coffee. It's caffeine free. It also works well with meats such as venison, kangaroo or even beef.

Wild meat

Protected species in Australia cannot be hunted for recreation. However, kangaroo is now available in supermarkets and most seafood is widely available. Plants and herbs can be sourced in your own garden or through markets and specialty suppliers.

Fish

Many fish species have catch limits and licences are required for fishing in most coastal areas. Catching your own fresh fish and cooking it is one of life's pleasures. Each state or territory in Australia maintains controls to protect fish species. There are legal size limits or 'bag limits' which are usually displayed on signage in popular fishing places and tackle shops. Fish species such as barramundi and crayfish and calamari are generally available throughout Australia

Blue Swimmer Crab

Blue swimmer crabs are widely distributed throughout the Pacific region and, in Australia, are found from Perth all the way around to southern New South Wales.

They live in a wide range of bays, estuaries and continental shelf areas to depths of 60 metres and prefer muddy or sandy bottoms.

Blue swimmer crabs make superb eating. They have a sweet, nutty flavour with a firm, moist and evenly textured flesh which is ideal for pastas, soups, crab cakes, or even in stir-fry's or salads. The meat is translucent when raw but turns white when cooked. The shell turns a bright orange colour making it a fantastic garnish.

Kangaroo

Kangaroo meat is rapidly becoming a common ingredient in the Australian diet and is being sought on supermarket shelves all over the country. It is sold all over the world, including Germany, Switzerland, Belgium and England.

Kangaroo meat sold commercially is only hunted by professional and licensed people and the carcass is inspected by qualified veterinarians before being passed for human consumption.

Kangaroo is very lean with only a 2% fat content and it is also high in protein, iron and zinc making it healthier than most other red meats. It is available in a number of different cuts depending on your intended use.

Due to the low fat content, kangaroo must be cooked very quickly. It is best seared in a hot pan and cooked nothing past medium-rare. Medium is tolerable but rare is best. Anything past medium-rare will start to dry out the meat, making it tough and very unpalatable. However, you can marinate the kangaroo in olive oil to gain some moisture which will allow you to cook it more. And of course, if you are using it in a stew or casserole it will not matter about the cooking time as it will take on the juices from the dish.

Ostrich

Ostriches are the largest flightless bird native to Africa and can grow up to 2.75 metres tall and weigh up to 156.5 kilograms with the ability to run up to 74 km/h. They are farmed all around the world for their feathers, skin and meat.

In comparison with other meat, ostrich is a nutritional, healthy choice with the meat being lean and low in cholesterol with only one third the content of beef fat—a great choice for the health conscious.

It has a delicate flavour that doesn't require marinades or herbs. Due to its low fat content it should not be cooked past medium as it will dry out and become flavourless.

Crocodile

When we think of crocodile we think of fierce creatures feeding on anything that gets in their way. This may be the reason why some people are nervous about trying this wonderful meat.

Crocodile has a unique texture that is available in a variety of cuts, the most popular being the tail. Croc legs and croc ribs are quite commonly used too. It has a taste that's quite similar to pork or chicken.

Croc meat is very versatile and can be grilled, fried, barbecued and even stewed. Crocodile is very healthy as it is low in fat, low in calories and high in protein, and is also a good source of niacin. It makes a great alternative to garlic prawns or smoked salmon and is an outstanding light and fresh dish for the hot weather.

The best way to cook crocodile is to keep it plain and simple. It goes well with lemon myrtle or lemon aspen and the ribs are great with a barbecue marinade—cooked similar to pork ribs.

When cooking the tail fillet, it should be seared off quickly and treated like a prawn. Do not overcook the meat as it will become tough and dry. It is best served with a light salad as an entrée.

Starters

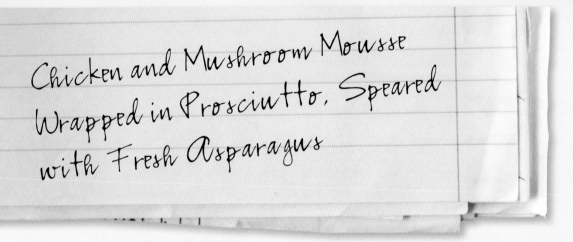

Chicken and Mushroom Mousse Wrapped in Prosciutto, Speared with Fresh Asparagus

Serves 2 as an entrée

100g mushrooms
1 chicken breast
4 egg whites
¾ cup cream
2 teaspoons salt
½ teaspoon pepper
8 slices of prosciutto
2 asparagus spears

Roughly chop the mushrooms and cook with the butter and thyme in a saucepan until soft, refrigerate until cold. Clean the chicken breast of any skin, bone and fat and chop roughly.

Blitz the chicken in a food processor until finely minced. Add the mushrooms and puree until smooth. Mushrooms must be chilled to prevent the next step from splitting. Pour in the egg whites and cream and combine well.

Mix in the salt and pepper.

Lay out a sheet of plastic wrap on the bench about the size of an open A4 notebook. Now lay another piece on top of this to double the thickness.

Lay the prosciutto in front of you on the plastic wrap, end to end, next to each other. Now repeat this working away from you to create a 2 x 4 pattern making sure all sides are overlapping, leaving a border of the plastic wrap around the prosciutto.

Now spread the chicken mix evenly onto the prosciutto mat leaving the top quarter uncovered. Trim the asparagus at both ends and lay in a line in the centre of the chicken mix.

Now carefully roll this towards the back using the plastic wrap for assistance. Much the same as rolling sushi. Use the uncovered quarter of the prosciutto to help join the roll together and wrap with the plastic wrap.

Grab the excess plastic on each end and roll across the bench until tight. Fold the 2 ends over and wrap one more time to secure together.

Now place in a steamer for 15 minutes.

You can also use a cake tin with a cake rack on the stove filled with a little water and covered with foil.

Sit for 10 minutes and then cut into wheels remembering to remove the plastic wrap. And if you're lucky, the asparagus might even be in the centre.

Red Bull Granita Oysters

Granita is an easy and tasty treat perfect for those warmer days that doesn't require any special equipment.

Serves 2 as an entrée

½ cup water
¼ cup sugar
1½ cans of Red Bull soft drink
12 oysters

Bring the water and sugar to the boil and cool to room temperature.

Stir in the red bull and then pour into a small baking pan and place into the freezer.

Every twenty minutes take the pan out and scrape the frozen mixture with a fork until all the frozen pieces are broken into small shavings and mixed well with the remaining liquid. Continue to freeze, scraping every twenty minutes until no more liquid is in the granita.

Now take a teaspoon and scoop a generous 'curl' of granita and place on the fresh oyster. Eat immediately.

Champagne Jelly Oysters

Serves 2 as an entrée

2 gelatine leaves
200ml champagne
12 oysters

Warm champagne in a saucepan and add gelatine leaf.

Remove from heat and stir until dissolved. Pour into a mould and chill for 3-4 hours.

To make different colours add a shot of liqueur such as Midori, Blue Curacao, etc. Roughly mix together some different colours with a fork.

Place a teaspoon of the jelly onto the fresh oyster and serve immediately.

Bacon Wrapped Tempura Oysters

Serves 2 as an entrée

1 cup flour
¼ cup cornstarch
1 teaspoon baking soda
¾ cup cold water
100g streaky bacon
12 oysters

Sift flours and baking soda into a bowl and mix in the water to form a batter consistency.

The cold water will enable the batter to 'explode' in the oil resulting in a light finish.

Wrap a small piece of bacon around the oyster and hold in place with a toothpick.

Heat a pot of oil to 180°C. This can be tested by placing a cube of bread into the oil and it should turn golden brown within 10 seconds.

Dip the oyster in the batter and then hold in the oil for ten seconds. slide the oyster off the toothpick with the back of a knife and continue to cook until golden brown.

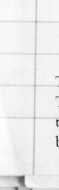

Oysters Kilpatrick

This is a slightly altered recipe from the original Kilpatrick sauce. The bacon has been replaced with chorizo, a spicy pork sausage typically from Spain and the barbecue sauce adds a more flavoursome background as opposed to the tomato sauce.

Serves 2 as an entrée

12 oysters
5 tablespoons Worcestershire sauce
5 tablespoons barbecue sauce
several drops of Tabasco sauce
(optional)
200g diced chorizo

Combine the liquid ingredients.

Generously sprinkle a baking tray with rock salt and place oysters on the salt.

Top oyster with diced chorizo and then a drizzle of the sauce.

Place under the grill and grill until crisp. Serve with a wedge of lemon.

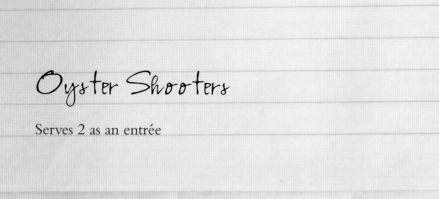

Oyster Shooters

Serves 2 as an entrée

Bloody Mary Oyster Shooters

6 oysters
100ml tomato juice
60ml vodka
2 teaspoons Worcestershire sauce
2 drops Tabasco sauce
cracked black pepper
celery stick

Combine tomato juice, vodka, Worcestershire sauce and Tabasco.
Place an oyster in a shot glass and fill with the bloody mary mix.
Cut the celery into small double matchstick-sized pieces. Top with freshly cracked black pepper and put in a stick of celery.

Vodka and Lime Oyster Shooters

150ml vodka
juice of 2 limes
6 oysters

Combine vodka and juice of lime and place in a shot glass with an oyster. Garnish with a slice of lime.

Gin and Lemon Oyster Shooters

6 oysters
150ml gin
juice of 1 large lemon

Combine gin and juice of lemon and place in a shot glass with an oyster. Garnish with a slice of lemon.

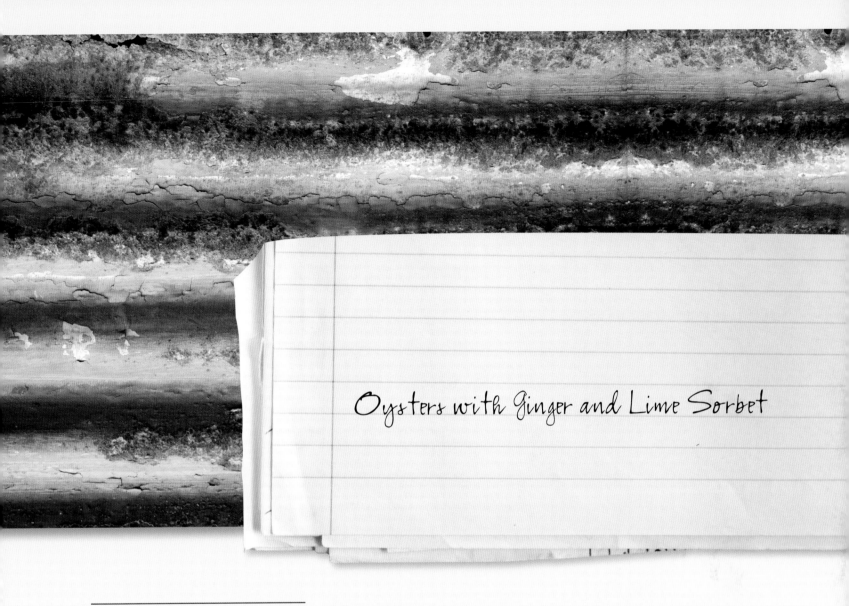

Oysters with Ginger and Lime Sorbet

12 oysters
2½ cups water
1 cup sugar
1½ tablespoons fresh ginger, peeled and finely chopped
1½ teaspoons finely grated lime peel
1½ tablespoons fresh lime juice

Combine water, sugar and ginger in a saucepan. Bring to boil, stirring until sugar dissolves. Reduce heat and simmer for 10 minutes. Strain liquid into a large bowl.

Return liquid to same saucepan. Add lime peel and boil for 2 minutes. Remove from heat. Whisk in lime juice then cool completely.

Pour mixture into an ice-cream machine and freeze according to manufacturer's instructions. Spoon the sorbet into a freezer-safe container; cover and freeze for 1 hour or until firm.

If you don't have an ice-cream machine, pour mixture into a baking tray and stir the sorbet every half hour to break up the ice crystals. You may have to run it through the blender if it freezes too solid or if it separates into its components.

Dip a teaspoon into hot water and scoop a generous 'curl' of the sorbet and place into the oyster. Serve immediately.

Witchetty Grub

Indigenous Australians have been eating these grubs for years and regard them as a delicacy, both good tasting and a great source of nutrition.

The taste is quite pleasant, having a fried egg flavour with a hint of nuts, and the skin resembles that of fried chicken skin.

The grubs live about 60cm below the ground and feed on the roots of trees, in particular the red river gum and the black wattle tree. They can usually be spotted by a small ring of sawdust and dirt at the base of the tree and can be caught by pushing a long piece of wire with a backward facing hook down the hole and just pulling them back out.

The grubs grow to about 7cm in length and are known to be high in protein. It is said that 10 witchetty grubs are sufficient to provide the daily protein needs of an adult.

The grub can be eaten raw, but if you wish to cook them the best way is to sear them all over in a hot pan until brown, the barbecue is perfect for this. You could try cooking them with some butter and even some garlic.

Poached Quail Eggs with Hollandaise Sauce

Quail eggs are considered a delicacy in many countries. They have a wonderful speckled shell making it great for a garnish and the eggs are terrific for an appetiser. You can generally use them in any way you would a chicken egg but they are often very high in cholesterol. Typically five quail eggs equal one chicken egg.

Quail eggs are quite tough to break so I suggest to crack the eggs into a small cup before placing them into the water.

Fill a deep frying pan with water, 2 tablespoons of vinegar and 1 tablespoon of salt. Bring to the boil and then reduce heat to a very low simmer.

Carefully crack eggs into the water and cook for 1 minute. They cook very quick so keep an eye on them.

Place eggs onto the toast circles and top with a dollop of hollandaise sauce (see below). You can even make Eggs Benedict by placing a small amount of ham underneath the egg or even Eggs Florentine by wilting some spinach with butter and placing it under the egg.

Toast

Cut out even circles of bread with a cutter, about 4 per slice, and grill each side under the grill until golden brown.

Hollandaise Sauce

Serves 2 with sauce for 12 eggs

4 tablespoons water
4 tablespoons white wine vinegar
4 black peppercorns
1 bayleaf
200g unsalted butter
2 egg yolks

Combine water, vinegar, pepper and bayleaf in a small saucepan and bring to the boil. Reduce heat and simmer until liquid is reduced to 2 tablespoons. Strain and cool down.

Melt the butter in a small saucepan over low heat. Use a metal spoon to skim any foam from the surface. Pour the clear yellow butter into a jug and discard the milky residue.

Combine egg yolks and vinegar mixture in a large heatproof bowl. Place over a saucepan of simmering water but do not allow water to touch base of bowl. Whisk mixture until it turns a pale yellow colour and thickened. Remove bowl from heat.

Gradually add melted butter in a thin, steady stream, whisking until mixture has thickened. If sauce becomes too thick, whisk in 1-2 tablespoons of hot water.

Spiced Quail Eggs

Serves 2

1 dozen quail eggs
1 tablespoon pistachio nuts, crushed
1 tablespoon macadamia nuts, crushed
2 teaspoons chopped parsley
1 teaspoon sea salt
1 teaspoon cracked black pepper

Bring a saucepan of water to the boil.
Carefully place eggs into the water and cook for 4 minutes.
Remove eggs and run under cold water for 5 minutes. Peel.
Combine remaining ingredients and then toss through the eggs.

Chilled Soup Shots

Chilled soups are a wonderful and interesting change for the summer months.
They are very simple to prepare and serve great as canapés or as an entree giving
the guest a selection of exciting flavour bursts leading up to their main course.

Serves 4. Each soup makes 12 shots

Watermelon, Cucumber, Red Onion and Mint Soup

½ cucumber, peeled and de-seeded	Blitz cucumber in a food processor until pureed.
2 cups of diced seedless watermelon	Add watermelon and red onion and puree until smooth.
½ teaspoon red onion, finely diced	Add mint and mix briefly.
2 large leaves of mint, chopped	Chill.

Rockmelon and Champagne Soup with Prosciutto Dust

2 egg yolks
45ml champagne
1/3 rockmelon, peeled, de-seeded
and roughly diced
1 thin slice prosciutto

Place yolks and champagne into a bowl and place over a pot of steaming water.

Whisk continuously until the yolks thicken and lighten in colour. Remove from heat.

Puree the rockmelon in a food processor and add to the yolks, combine well then chill.

Place the prosciutto in the oven for about 5 minutes at 180°C until it goes crisp. Remove and let cool.

Crush the prosciutto until it resembles a dust and sprinkle on top of the soup before serving.

Soup shots from left to right: Watermelon, Cucumber, Red Onion and Mint;
Rockmelon and Champagne; Avocado; and Tomato, Chilli and Coconut

Avocado Soup

1 avocado	Peel avocado and remove seed. Dice into chunks.
1 teaspoon lemon juice	Puree in a food processor with the lemon juice then add the milk.
1 cup of milk	Mix in the salt and pepper.
1 teaspoon salt	Chill.
½ teaspoon Szechuan pepper	

Tomato, Chilli and Coconut Soup

½ onion, finely diced	Cook onion in a saucepan until it turns transparent with little colour.
1 clove garlic, crushed	Add garlic and cook for 2 minutes.
1 birds-eye chilli, chopped	Add chilli and cook for a further 2 minutes then add white wine.
60ml white wine	Add tomatoes and cook for 3 minutes then add the flour and stir in well.
2 tomatoes, roughly chopped and core removed	Add water and coconut milk and bring to the boil.
2 teaspoons plain flour	Reduce heat to a slow simmer and cook for 10 minutes.
1 cup water	Puree in a food processor or with a stick blender until smooth.
½ cup coconut milk	Season to taste.
salt and pepper	Pass through a sieve to remove any lumps. Chill.
	This soup is also great served hot.

Simple Bread Recipe

This is a basic bread recipe that can be used in a number of different ways. It can be used to make big chunky loaves or rolled into baguettes or even into crispy flat-bread.

Makes one loaf

1kg plain flour
20g yeast
20g sugar
20g salt
3-4 cups of lukewarm water

It is essential that the water is lukewarm, approximately 30°C, as this temperature will encourage the yeast to grow. If it is too hot it will kill the yeast and if it is too cold it will not activate. The yeast works by fermenting when warmed causing carbon dioxide to be produced and trapped in the dough as small air bubbles which cause the bread to rise during cooking.

Place dry ingredients into a mixer with a dough hook and mix well to combine. Slowly add water until dough is sticky and light. Knead for 8-10 minutes.

Alternatively, place dry ingredients into a bowl and mix well. Make a well in the centre and slowly add the water incorporating it in with a wooden spoon. Bring the dough together with your hands then transfer onto a floured bench. Knead for 8-10 minutes. This part is important as kneading helps distribute the yeast evenly through the dough and develops and strengthens the gluten in the flour which will determine the success of the final result. Once kneaded, the dough should be elastic and smooth.

Place into a clean large bowl and lightly cover with a damp tea-towel. Place in a warm spot (around 30°C) to 'prove' for an hour until dough doubles in size.

Once doubled in size, hit the dough in the centre. This is called 'knocking back' and will release any excess carbon dioxide that has been produced by the yeast during the proving process and will prevent a strong yeasty taste. The dough will collapse in size at this stage.

Turn dough onto a floured bench and knead for 2 more minutes until smooth. Portion dough into 6 even-sized pieces then roll into balls. Place onto a floured tray and let sit, covered with a damp tea-towel for approximately 30 minutes.

Cook in a 200°C pre-heated oven for 30 minutes until golden brown and bread makes a hollow sound when knocked on the bottom with your knuckles. Cool on a wire rack.

Variations

• Add some freshly chopped herbs to the flour mixture such as rosemary, parsley and chives.
• Add some chopped olives and sun-dried tomatoes.
• Roll flat and drizzle with olive oil and sprinkle with sea salt and cracked black pepper.
• Add some walnuts and sultanas for a fruit-n-nut variety.
• Add some roasted garlic for a twist on garlic bread.

Dukkah

Dukkah is an Egyptian blend of nuts, seeds and Middle Eastern spices. It is commonly eaten by dipping a piece of bread in good olive oil then into the dukkah and served as a pre-dinner appetiser or as a snack. It can also be used as a crust for meats such as fish and chicken and it also works well as a seasoning for lamb.

Makes 2 cups. Serves 6

Lemon Myrtle and Pepperberry Dukkah

1 cup sliced almonds
3 tablespoons sesame seeds
1 tablespoon coriander seeds
1 tablespoon mustard seeds
1 teaspoon fennel seeds
1 tablespoon ground lemon myrtle
1 teaspoon ground pepperberry
1 teaspoon good sea salt flakes

Preheat oven to 180°C.

Spread almonds evenly on a large baking tray and roast for 3-4 minutes until golden brown. Stir occasionally to assist in even cooking. Blitz in a food processor until coarsely chopped and transfer to a large mixing bowl.

Cook the sesame seeds in a dry frypan for 1-2 minutes, tossing regularly until golden brown. Add to the almonds.

Separately cook the coriander, mustard and fennel seeds in a dry frypan for 1-2 minutes until fragrant. Pound in a mortar and pestle to crush the seeds.

Add seeds to the almonds along with the lemon myrtle, pepperberry and sea salt. Mix well and store in an air-tight container at room temperature.

Macadamia and Saltbush Dukkah

1 cup chopped macadamia nuts
3 tablespoons sesame seeds
1 tablespoon coriander seeds
1 tablespoon mustard seeds
2 teaspoons cumin seeds
1 teaspoon fennel seeds
1 tablespoon saltbush, ground
1 teaspoon freshly ground black pepper

Preheat oven to 180°C. Roast macadamia nuts for 3-4 minutes until golden brown. Stir occasionally to assist in even cooking. Blitz in food processor until coarsely chopped and transfer to large mixing bowl.

Cook the sesame seeds in a dry frypan for 1-2 minutes tossing regularly until golden brown. Add to the nuts.

Separately cook the coriander, mustard, cumin and fennel seeds in a dry frypan for 1-2 minutes until fragrant. Pound in a mortar and pestle to crush the seeds.

Add seeds to the nuts along with the saltbush and ground pepper. Mix well and store in an air-tight container at room temperature.

Dips

Dips are great for using up leftovers or even to create a masterpiece. Cream cheese bases are popular, but they can also be made from cooked pumpkin, sweet potato, fresh crushed tomato, sour cream, avocado, eggplant or mayonnaise. Serve with bush damper (see next recipe) for a great starter.

Serves 4. Makes 1½–2 cups

Bush Tomato Dip

200g cream cheese
4 tablespoons dried bush tomato
10 sundried tomatoes, finely chopped
1 small garlic clove, finely crushed
cracked pepperberry
salt

Mix all ingredients together in a food processor until well combined. Serve at room temperature.

Caramelised Red Onion Dip

1 large red onion
80ml balsamic vinegar
150g cream cheese
salt to taste.
cracked black pepper

Thinly slice red onion. Sauté in a frypan on medium heat to cook with little colour.

When soft, increase heat then add balsamic vinegar and cook for 1 minute. Let cool.

Mix onion with cream cheese and add salt and pepper. Serve at room temperature.

Beetroot Dip

250g cream cheese
1 large beetroot
1 tablespoon red wine vinegar
½ teaspoon chopped fresh chilli
salt to taste

Boil whole, unpeeled beetroot in salted water for 30-60 minutes making sure to keep covered with water. The beetroot will be cooked when a knife will slide easily into it holding no resistance when pulled out.

Peel the beetroot and puree in a food processor until smooth then refrigerate until cold.

Return to the food processor and add the chilli and puree for 1 minute.

Add the cream cheese and red wine vinegar and combine well.

Salt to taste.

Serve at room temperature.

Spiced Pumpkin Dip

750g butternut pumpkin, peeled and cut into chunks
½ teaspoon nutmeg
1 teaspoon cumin
1 teaspoon crushed ginger
1 clove garlic, crushed
salt and pepper to taste
125g smooth ricotta cheese
½ teaspoon chilli powder

Toss the pumpkin with nutmeg, cumin, ginger, garlic, salt and pepper with a little oil.

Roast in the oven at 180°C for 30-40 minutes until soft.

Puree in a food processor until smooth then stir through the ricotta cheese and chilli powder.

Bush Damper

Damper was developed back in the settlement days of Australia when stockmen had only sacks of flour and campfires to cure their hunger.

Traditionally it is made out of flour, water and salt and baked in the coals of the campfire or wrapped around a stick and baked in an open fire. These days damper can comfortably be made at home but is much better over a wood fire where you will get that rustic smokey flavour through the bread.

You can also add optional ingredients to this recipe such as fruit, nuts or cheese. You can even try a dash of your favourite beer.

Makes one loaf

4 cups self-raising flour
3 tablespoons butter, room temperature
¾ cup water
¾ cup milk
1 teaspoon salt

Sift flour and then rub in the butter until a breadcrumb texture forms.

Form a well in the top of the flour, pour in the water and milk, and mix well.

Add any extra ingredients now if desired.

Knead until smooth using a dusting of flour to help.

Shape into 6-8 small balls and bake on a floured tray in a pre-heated oven for 40-50 minutes at 180°C.

When cooked, they should give a hollow sound when knocked on the bottom.

To cook in the campfire, pull some hot coals aside and place dough either on top or even bury it in the coals. Rub off any ash before eating.

Alternatively, wrap the dough around a stick and rest on the side of the fire and rotate periodically.

Wattleseed Crusted Venison with Fig Compote and Chocolate Red Wine Sauce

Venison has a strong game flavour that is similar to a strong beef or kangaroo. It is very lean therefore should not be cooked past medium to prevent it drying out and becoming tough and flavourless. Venison is lower in calories and cholesterol than most other popular cuts of meat. It is also a great source of potassium, niacin, zinc and iron.

It takes on the flavour of the wattleseed very well, adding a nutty background. This is highly complimented by the bitterness of the red wine chocolate sauce being backed up by the fig compote. The texture of the wattleseed also adds a great character with a slight grainy feel. It is recommended that this dish is followed with a sorbet to break down the sweet finish.

Serves 4

Fig compote
200g dried figs
75g brown sugar
75ml balsamic vinegar
½ cup of water

Chocolate red wine sauce
100ml red wine
100ml cream
125g dark cooking chocolate, chopped (or buttons)

4 fresh figs
900g venison fillet
50g ground wattleseed

For the fig compote, finely slice the figs and place into a saucepan with the brown sugar. Cook on a medium heat for 10 minutes until the sugar has melted and the liquid has reduced in size.

Add the balsamic vinegar and simmer until the liquid has reduced to half the volume. Add the water and continue to cook until it resembles a chunky jam consistency. Let cool. If compote seems too thick, just add some more water.

In a saucepan, heat the red wine and simmer until it has reduced to a third of its original volume. Light with a flame and wait until it burns out. This will burn the alcohol off leaving the behind the taste of the wine. Add the cream and bring to the boil. Reduce heat and simmer for 3 minutes. Remove from heat and stir in the chocolate until completely combined.

To cook the venison, roll the meat in the wattleseed without covering too thickly, as the wattleseed can prove to be quite strong. Seal the meat all sides and finish in the oven until medium-rare.

To serve, cut a fresh fig into quarters keeping the bottom intact. Place the fig compote into the fig. Slice the venison into several pieces and fan out in front of the fig. Drizzle with the sauce.

Vegemite Soup

As strange as it may sound, this is a very delicious soup that is quite filling and easy to make. It's perfect for those days when you open your cupboard doors to reveal bare shelves full of dust and spider webs.

Vegemite is a great source of vitamins, in particular the B group which includes thiamine, riboflavin, niacin, folate, pantothenic acid, pyridoxine, biotin and p-amino benzoic acid, which are all extremely beneficial for cell and nerve production, as well as a healthy digestive system and skin and eyes. Just one slice of bread with vegemite can provide a high percentage of most of these daily requirements.

Just spread generously 2-3 slices of bread with vegemite. Tear into several pieces and place into a bowl. Pour over some boiling water until the bread is covered and let sit for 3 minutes. Whisk with a fork to break apart the bread and serve.

Great for a cold winter's day.

Rabbit Ravioli
with Horseradish Custard, Caramelised Orange Sauce and Shredded Snowpeas

Rabbit is a healthy alternative to white meat being extremely lean and a great source of high quality protein. It has been a part of the European and English diet for centuries and it now holds a regular spot in the Australian culture.

Rabbit can be cooked in various ways including boiling, braising, frying, baking, grilling and barbecuing and can be used in most ways chicken meat is used. It is quite commonly made into a stew.

This ravioli dish is designed to be eaten by having a bit of everything on your fork as the sweetness of the sauce with the tartness of the horseradish and the texture of the snowpeas provide an amazing combination in your mouth.

This dish is also perfect using duck.

Roasted rabbit

1 rabbit
¼ cup olive oil
salt and pepper
6 sprigs thyme
2 cloves garlic, crushed, whole
¼ cup dry white wine

Preheat oven to 160°C.

Rub rabbit with the oil and sprinkle with salt and pepper.

Place into a roasting pan and add thyme and garlic.

Roast for half hour then pour the wine into the pan then baste the rabbit with the juices.

Baste the rabbit every 15 minutes for the next 1 hour until golden brown.

Pasta

1 egg
1 egg yolk
200g plain flour
2 tablespoons salt
1 teaspoon olive oil

Combine all ingredients in a food processor until they come together.

Tip onto a floured bench and knead for 5 minutes.

Now wrap in plastic wrap and let sit in the fridge for 2 hours.

It is essential that you rest the pastry to prevent it shrinking and becoming tough.

Sauce

2 large juicy oranges
¼ cup sugar
2 tablespoons butter
1 tablespoons chopped parsley

Cut the oranges in half and grill in a pan, skin facing up, until they turn a deep brown colour.

Squeeze the juice through a strainer into a saucepan and add the sugar.

Bring to the boil and reduce until it is half the original volume.

Remove from heat and whisk the butter into the juice.

Add parsley.

Ravioli

200g roasted rabbit meat
2 tablespoons sour cream
Salt and pepper to taste

Mix together the rabbit meat, sour cream, salt and pepper. Roll out the pastry until it is very thin and cut out 8cm diameter circles. Place 2 teaspoons of mixture in the centre of each circle.

Beat an egg and brush the edges of the pastry.

Now pick up a single ravioli in both hands, fold and lightly squeeze together the edges making sure all air is squeezed from the inside. This is essential as any air will cause the ravioli to break during the cooking process. Now give the edges a firm press.

Bring a pot of salted water to the boil then reduce heat to a simmer.

Place ravioli in the water one after the other without over-crowding the pot and cook for 5 minutes.

Remove from pot, straining well, and toss into the orange sauce.

Horseradish custard

300ml milk
2 eggs
1 egg yolk
1 tablespoon crushed horseradish
1 teaspoon salt

Whisk the eggs, yolk, horseradish and salt until well combined.

Warm the milk and stir (not whisk) into the egg mix. Let sit for 5 minutes. Preheat oven to 120°C.

Strain then pour into five small greased moulds.

Place on a tray and bake in the oven for 15-20 minutes

15 snowpeas, sliced on 45 degree angle

Place the custard in the middle of the plate. Arrange the ravioli around the custard and drizzle with some extra sauce. Garnish with snowpeas on top of the custard.

Lemon Myrtle Crusted Crocodile

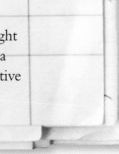

Crocodile and lemon myrtle go well together. The bushy lemon flavour matches the light sweet flavour of the crocodile. Grilling the lemon myrtle adds a very slight smokey flavour to the dish as well. The daikon radish and cucumber salad makes a perfect addition providing a great dimension to the dish by adding a salty alternative with a slight Asian flavour.

Serves 4

Salad
½ daikon radish
½ cucumber
2 tablespoons soy sauce
2 tablespoons brown sugar

500g crocodile tail
2 teaspoons ground lemon myrtle

Peel then slice the daikon radish into 'slightly larger than matchstick' size pieces.

Cut the cucumber the same but discard the centre keeping the skin on.

Place in separate bowls and sprinkle them with a generous amount of salt and let sit for 10 minutes to extract the liquid.

Now wash off the salt with some water and marinate the daikon in the soy and brown sugar and roast on a tray for approximately 15 minutes at 180°C.

Wash the cucumber and toss through the cooked daikon radish.

For the crocodile, gently roll into the lemon myrtle lightly covering the outside.

Cut into bite-sized medallions and grill each side in a hot pan, being careful not to over-cook.

This will serve 2-4 people and is great for an entree and a perfect alternative to garlic prawns or smoked salmon.

Crocodile Legs

Crocodile legs hold a strange resemblance to tip-less chicken wings, only bigger, meatier and with a distinct sweet pork flavour. The first impression of the flesh is that it's going to be really tough but the second that you sink your teeth into these, you will discover complete tenderness and juicy flavoursome meat.

Crocodile legs make wonderful finger food and would go great with a barbecue marinade or even a lemon mix, especially lemon myrtle.

And there's definitely an eerie feeling about sitting at the bar munching on a croc leg while enjoying a nice cold one, especially if you're sitting in the tropics.

Simple Grilled Crocodile Legs

Cut crocodile legs in half and sprinkle with salt and pepper.
Grill in a hot pan until they start to brown and then place into the oven at 160°C for 10 minutes.
If you marinate them, place them straight in the oven for 15 minutes.

Abalone

Abalone are basically large marine snails which feed on algae. They have a large muscular foot that clings to rocks in the ocean and they will usually stay fixed in the one spot. The abalone will grow according to the tidal flow in the area and the number of algae drifting past.

Abalone meat has long been considered a delicacy in various parts of the world and some cultures consider it to be a symbol of wealth and prestige. It grows all over the globe, and Tasmania provides approximately 25 per cent of the annual world abalone harvest.

There are many ways to cook abalone and a lot of people try to experiment by adding other ingredients and using different preparations and cooking methods but I find by keeping it simple you will get the full experience and flavour of the abalone. To successfully cook abalone it should be cut thin and cooked quickly. Beating the meat is not necessary. Once cleaned, slice horizontally into 5mm thicknesses. Lightly season with salt and sear in a hot pan with a little oil. Cook for 30 seconds each side, long enough to create some colour then serve immediately. Drizzle with some fresh lemon juice if desired. Do not over cook as it will become very tough and dry.

The shell also provides an attractive piece that is commonly made into jewellery, buttons, carvings and even as an inlay for furniture or musical instruments such as guitars. It is also not unusual to see an abalone shell being used as an ashtray.

Snails

When we think of the traditional *escargot* our minds automatically travel to France but snail farming in Australia is rapidly growing and is sure to create a huge market in the future for the experimental consumer.

Traditionally, they are served with lots of garlic butter. Place some butter into the shell then press the snail into the butter and then top with more garlic butter. Place into a 200°C oven for about 5 minutes, just enough time to melt the butter and serve immediately with bread.

Snails are available in cans ready to use but they can also be cooked easily from fresh. To do this they need to be cooked in a court-bouillon for 60-90 minutes depending on their size.

Serves 1

Court bouillon
30 snails
½ litre white wine
2 litres water
1 bunch of parsley stalks
5 sprigs thyme
4 shallots, chopped roughly
4 cloves garlic, crushed, whole
1 carrot, roughly chopped
2 sticks celery, roughly chopped
2 bayleaves
2 tablespoons of salt
20 peppercorns

Place all ingredients into a pot with the snails and bring to the boil.

Reduce heat to a light simmer and cook for 60-90 minutes until they become tender.

Gourmet Snails

This dish holds on to the traditional method of lots of garlic and butter, but provides a tastier and fresher finish.

Serves 1

1 tablespoon crushed garlic
100ml white wine
20ml white wine vinegar
1 teaspoon fresh tarragon, chopped
8 pre-cooked snails
75g butter, diced
½ Roma tomato, de-seeded, diced
handful of wild rocket leaves

Cook crushed garlic in oil in a warm frypan and heat until the garlic starts to cook without any colour.

Just before it starts to brown, hit it with the white wine and reduce to half original volume. Add a splash of white wine vinegar then toss in some fresh tarragon.

Add the snails and cook for long enough to warm them through.

Remove from heat and add some cubes of butter and toss around until it combines. This will produce a nice sauce.

Toss in the diced tomato flesh and some picked wild rocket and season with sea salt. Serve with thinly sliced toast.

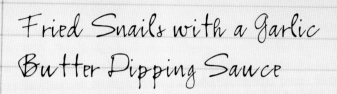

Fried Snails with a garlic Butter Dipping Sauce

This is a great introduction to snails, especially for people that don't like looking at them.

Serves 2

1 egg
1 cup milk
10 pre-cooked snails
½ cup breadcrumbs
¼ cup plain flour

Dipping sauce
1 tablespoon crushed garlic
50ml white wine
100ml cream
75g butter, diced

Place the flour and the breadcrumbs into two separate bowls.

Combine the egg and milk and place into a third bowl.

Roll the snails in the flour until lightly covered. Shake off excess flour.

Submerge into egg and milk mixture until all covered in the liquid.

Remove from liquid and drain briefly then place into breadcrumbs.

Roll around until completely covered then remove, shaking off excess crumbs.

Heat a pot of oil to 180°C. This can be tested by placing a cube of bread into the oil and it should turn golden brown within 10 seconds.

Place snails into the oil for 2-3 minutes until they turn golden brown.

To prepare the dipping sauce, cook crushed garlic in oil in a warm saucepan and heat until the garlic starts to cook without any colour. Add white wine and cook for 1 minute.

Add the cream, cook gently and reduce until it reaches half of the original volume.

Remove from heat and stir in the diced butter until completely combined.

Season with salt and pepper to taste.

Serve fried snails warm with dipping sauce on the side.

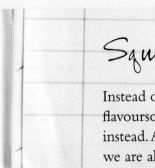

Squid

Instead of the traditional fried variety, I add a healthier twist to this flavoursome dish by keeping all the expected flavours and stuffing it instead. And for those who want tradition, there is also a recipe that we are all used to.

Salt and Pepper Stuffed Baby Calamari

Serves 4-6

150g chicken mince
100g white fish, minced
4 egg whites, lightly beaten
1 tablespoon cracked black pepper
1 tablespoon lemon pepper
2 tablespoons sea salt
rind of ½ lemon, finely grated
¼ cup cream
1kg baby squid tubes

Citrus salad
2 oranges
2 grapefruit
1 lemon
4 limes
100g wild rocket leaves
60 ml olive oil

Combine all ingredients thoroughly, except the squid tubes, in a food processor. The mixture should be still moist but able to hold a shape.

Pipe or spoon the mixture into the tubes leaving a 1cm gap at the end of the tube as the stuffing will expand when cooked. Preheat oven to 180°C.

Place the stuffed squid into a deep tray (a cake tin is perfect) and add enough water to cover the bottom to about 1cm deep.

Bake for 10-15 minutes. The squid will feel quite firm when ready.

Try replacing the lemon pepper with some lemon myrtle instead.

Peel the fruit from the salad and cut out the segments with a sharp knife. Toss the rocket through and drizzle with oilive oil.

Sprinkle salad on top of squid to serve.

Traditional Salt and Pepper Calamari

Serves 4

½ cup corn flour
½ cup plain flour
2 tablespoons cracked black pepper
1 tablespoon lemon pepper
2 tablespoons sea salt
6 large squid tubes

Mix all ingredients together in a bowl.

Either cut squid tubes into rings, or for a better effect, cut the tube in half lengthways and then cut a criss-cross pattern on the inside of the tube. Now cut into smaller bite-sized pieces approx 3cm x 3cm. Heat some oil in a wok or saucepan until it reaches 180°C. A good way to test this is to place a cube of bread in the oil and it should turn golden brown within 10 seconds.

Now dust the squid pieces in the flour and shake off the excess. Fry for about 2 minutes and drain on some paper towel.

Moroccan Inspired Oven Roasted Quail on Pilaf Rice with a Mint Saffron Yoghurt

Serves 2

Quail

4 whole quail
2 teaspoon ground coriander
2 teaspoon ground cumin
2 teaspoon turmeric
1 teaspoon paprika
1 teaspoon crushed garlic
1 tablespoon lemon juice
¼ cup olive oil

Bone and trim the quail and keep all bones and off-cuts for the stock.

Combine all ingredients and rub into the quail. Marinate in fridge for 2-4 hours.

Pre-heat the oven to 200°C. Place on a tray and bake at 200°C for 12 minutes.

Rice

1 onion, diced
2 cloves garlic, crushed
1 cup rice
1.25 cups quail stock
½ carrot, small diced
1 stick celery, small diced
Rind and juice of ½ orange
salt

Make a quail stock by placing off-cuts of quail into a saucepan and covering with 1 litre of water. Bring to the boil and reduce to a slow simmer for 3 hours. Strain through a fine sieve.

Sweat off onion and garlic in a saucepan until soft with little colour. Pre-heat the oven to 160°C. Pile all ingredients including the onion mix and stock into a deep oven tray and cover with foil. Bake in oven for 20-25 minutes.

Mint and Saffron Dressing

0.2g saffron (1 fifth of a packet)
2 tablespoons hot water
½ cup Greek yoghurt
Juice of 1 small lemon
2 tablespoons chopped mint
1 teaspoon salt

Combine saffron with hot water and let sit for 5 minutes.

Now stir all ingredients together including the saffron mix.

To assemble: Carefully place the rice in the centre of the plate. Top with the quail and drizzle some dressing around the edge of the plate. Serve with some wilted bok-choy or spinach.

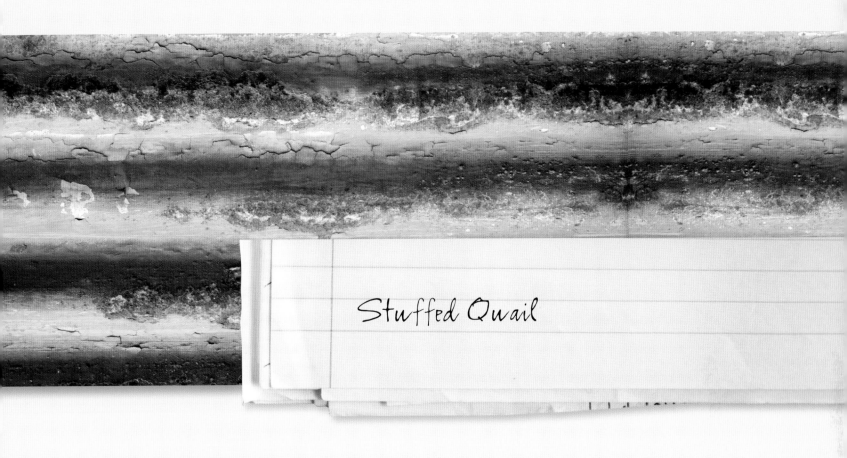

Stuffed Quail

Serves 4

½ onion, diced
2 cloves garlic, crushed
½ cup rice
¾ cup water
Rind and juice of half a lemon
Salt
cracked pepper
2 egg whites, lightly beaten
2 tablespoons chopped parsley
2 tablespoons grated Parmesan cheese
4 boneless quail
¼ cup macadamia nuts, roasted and crushed

Pre-heat oven to 180°C.

Sweat off onion and garlic in a saucepan until soft with little colour.

Place rice, water, lemon juice and rind, salt, pepper, and onion mix into a deep oven tray and cover with foil. Place in oven and cook for 20-25 minutes.

Stir with a fork and let sit for 15 minutes.

Now add the egg, parmesan, parsley and macadamia nuts.

Press together enough of the mix to fit inside the quail and hold together with either a skewer or truss it with some butchers twine.

Rub the outside with a little oil and bake in the oven for approximately 15 minutes.

To assemble: Slice the quail on an angle into 4-5 even pieces. Carefully place onto a plate still holding it together. Serve immediately.

Lemon Myrtle Smoked Chicken Turkish Sandwich with Mango Dressing

The mango dressing compliments the strong taste of the smoked chicken while the avocado and tomato enhances the flavours to provide a complete experience.

Serves 1

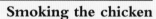

Smoking the chicken
1 chicken breast
2 tablespoons ground lemon myrtle

1 Turkish bread roll
1 smoked chicken breast
Tomato slices
Avocado slices
Lettuce
Mango dressing
Salt
Freshly cracked black pepper

There are two ways to smoke the chicken.

1. Slice chicken in half and place on a cake rack. Sprinkle lemon myrtle in an old cake tin and place the rack inside. This can also be done in a large frypan. Cover with foil and heat on the stove. The lemon myrtle will start to smoke within 30 seconds. Reduce heat to produce a slow steady smoking effect. Continue for 8 minutes and finish the cooking of the chicken in the oven if necessary.

2. Slice chicken in half and place on a cake rack. Sprinkle lemon myrtle directly onto the barbecue plate and place rack over the lemon myrtle. Cover with a metal bowl or some aluminium foil that has been shaped into a bowl. This can be done by moulding the foil over a mixing bowl. Smoke for 10 minutes or until the chicken is cooked.

Mango dressing
1 mango
½ teaspoon fresh lime juice
2 egg yolks
1 tablespoon Dijon mustard
1 tablespoon white wine vinegar
250ml vegetable oil
Salt and pepper

Puree mango and lime juice in a food processor or with a fork in a bowl, it doesn't have to be real smooth.

In a separate mixing bowl or food processor, whisk together egg yolks, mustard, vinegar and a quarter of the mango puree.

Slowly and steadily pour in the oil while vigorously whisking together.

Finally add the rest of the mango puree and season with salt and pepper to taste.

If dressing is too thick, add a little hot water to consistency.

To assemble: Cut the Turkish bread in half and layer all salad ingredients inside. Place the chicken on top and drizzle with a generous amount of mango dressing.

Roasted Baby Beetroot

Beetroot is one of those ingredients that often finds its way into tossed salads and salad sandwiches. It also works well with beef and is great on its own as a snack or entree.

Serves 2

1 bunch baby beetroot
¼ cup brown sugar
¼ cup balsamic vinegar

2 tablespoons balsamic vinegar
3 tablespoons castor sugar

Pre-heat oven to 160°C. Peel beetroot and cover and boil in water for 10 minutes. Strain liquid into a saucepan for the beetroot glaze.
   Combine sugar and vinegar and toss through the beetroot.
   Place on an oven tray and bake for 15-20 minutes.
   Keep turning and baste every 3-4 minutes.
   They will be ready when you insert a small sharp knife and it will pull out showing little resistance.

Beetroot glaze
Reduce liquid from beetroot until there is ½ cup left.
   Add 2 tablespoons balsamic vinegar and bring to the boil for 2 minutes.
   Add 3 tablespoons of castor sugar and bring to the boil.
   Reduce to a light simmer and cook for 5 minutes until it thickens.

Toss the cooked beetroot with the glaze and serve immediately.

Mussels

Mussels are found throughout the world in colonies along rocky shores creating beds of black sheets.

As well as being tasty, mussels provide a nutritious source of B and C vitamins, Omega 3 fatty acids, iron, magnesium, phosphorus, potassium, selenium and zinc.

They can be prepared in a number of ways such as smoked, boiled, steamed and fried and are quite often cooked with chilli and garlic for a starter or even a meal on their own. They are also great to throw fresh in the camp fire and removed as soon as they open. You will taste a slight smokey flavour along with the saltiness of the sea. The most important thing is to never overcook the mussels as they will shrivel and become rubbery.

Mussels should be alive just before they are cooked because they can quickly become toxic after they die. A quick tap on the outside of the shell will determine whether they are good to eat. If the mussel doesn't close then it is dead and should be discarded. Also, any unopened mussels after cooking should also be discarded. Before cooking, the mussels should have a thorough wash under cold water and the beard can be removed by giving a sharp pull towards the point of the mussel. Another rule is to avoid any mussels that are growing on wood as they can pick up poisonous toxins from the timber.

Creamy Garlic Mussels

Serves 4

6 cloves garlic, thinly sliced
1 tablespoon butter
2 dozen fresh black mussels
100ml white wine
180ml cream

In a large pot, soften the garlic in the butter.

Increase heat and add the mussels then cover and steam them open in their own juices for 3–4 minutes shaking the pot every now and then.

Remove mussels and add white wine and boil for 3–5 minutes until liquid has reduced to half of its original volume.

Add cream and boil for 3 minutes. Add mussels and toss through the sauce. Finish with some chopped parsley.

Try adding half of a thinly sliced leek with the garlic for a great alternative.

Yabbies

Yabbies are a type of small inland freshwater crayfish found in Australia. They are capable of living in virtually any body of fresh water including rivers, creeks, streams, lakes and dams. Yabbies are active burrowers and are able to withstand long periods of drought by burrowing deep into the soil until they reach moisture. Because of this, they have been known to cause considerable accidental damage by destroying banks and dam walls.

Yabbies are great eating having a very sweet and tender meat. They are available in multiple sizes and can be used in many ways. They are commonly served on seafood buffets, split and char-grilled, or served with chilli but the most popular is boiled then de-shelled and served on their own or in combination with pastas, salads, or even stir fries. They even make good bait for fishermen and have also made their way into fish tanks of keen pet owners.

The easiest and most humane way to kill yabbies, or any crustacean, is to chill them in the freezer for about 30 minutes or in the refrigerator for an hour until they become insensible. This will slow down their nervous system.

To cook the yabbies, bring a large pot of heavily salted water to a rolling boil. Place chilled yabbies into the boiling water for 2 minutes or until they turn completely orange. Remove from water and let cool.

Yabby Cocktail

This is a modern twist on the classic prawn cocktail served with fresh salad leaves and a cocktail dipping sauce.

Serves 4

2 egg yolks
1 tablespoon Dijon mustard
1 tablespoon fresh lemon juice
250ml vegetable oil
1 teaspoon crushed horseradish
2 tablespoons tomato sauce
1 tablespoon Worcestershire sauce
4–6 drops Tabasco sauce (optional)
salt and pepper
salad leaves
12 yabbies

In a mixing bowl or food processor, whisk together egg yolks, mustard and lemon juice.

Slowly and steadily pour in the oil while vigorously whisking together.

Add the horseradish, tomato sauce, Worcestershire sauce and optional Tobasco sauce then season with salt and pepper to taste.

If dressing is too thick, add a little hot water to consistency.

Remove yabby meat from shell and serve on fresh salad leaves with a generous serving of the cocktail sauce.

Marron Mornay

Marron are a type of freshwater crayfish predominately found in South-Western Australia. There are strict laws on catching marron due to the reduction in the marron population. Places where marron are found have been decreasing and they are vulnerable to several predators causing a concern for this amazing species. They have been introduced to other areas of Australia to increase development in the population and to sustain a steady supply for the future.

Marron make excellent eating with a flavour quite similar to crayfish although not usually as big. They can be cooked in a variety of ways such as boiling and grilling. To prepare the marron, the humane way to kill it is to chill them in the fridge for a few hours, then drop them headfirst into boiling water, or split them quickly with a large knife head to tail for recipes using the raw meat.

Serves 4

10 peppercorns
4 tablespoons salt
5 parsley stalks with no leaves
¼ fennel, sliced
4 marron

Chill the marron in the fridge for 2 hours or in the freezer for 15–20 minutes.

Place all ingredients into a large pot and fill with water. Bring to the boil. Drop the marron headfirst into the boiling water being careful not to overload the pot and cook for 5 minutes.

Remove then run under cold water for 2 minutes.

Mornay sauce
60g butter
1 tablespoon fresh lemon juice
3 cloves crushed garlic
60g flour
600ml full-cream milk
100g grated Parmesan cheese plus extra for garnish
chopped parsely to garnish

Melt butter in a saucepan with the lemon juice and garlic then add the flour.

Stir vigorously until combined and cook out for 2 minutes being careful to not let it stick.

Add the milk and bring to the boil, stirring continuously, then turn down to a simmer for 3–4 minutes.

Add parmesan cheese then salt and pepper to taste.

Add some chopped parsley if desired.

Try adding crushed macadamia nuts to the sauce for an added effect.

To finish

Remove the meat from the marron and dice into 1cm cubes. Mix with the mornay sauce then add back into the shell.

Sprinkle with some extra Parmesan cheese and place under the grill until golden brown.

Top with finely chopped parsley.

Herbs and micro herbs

There are hundreds of different kinds of herbs on the market and micro herbs are simply early versions of these. The herbs are usually harvested between 7-14 days and they are quite intense in flavour and packed full of nutrients. Chefs are using these herbs all over the world for many different dishes both savoury and sweet and they are also being used for great garnishes, replacing the dated parsley and rosemary. They have a very delicate visual appeal about them adding a fresh healthy addition to complete your evening.

Micro herbs can be used in soups, desserts, herb butter, herb tea, or substituted with usual herb varieties to add that special touch to your favourite dish. A herb salad is a great way to experience the true flavours that these herbs have to offer. When making a salad it is best to pick a selection of herbs with different flavours to balance each other out. Listed is a variety of commonly used micro herbs.

Chard: Bright red and green contrasted leaves with red stems and a light sweet flavour.

Lemon balm: Strong fresh zesty lemon taste and smell.

Mache: Otherwise known as Lamb's Tongue. Green velvety leaves with a bitter nutty flavour.

Mustard cress: Small green leaves with a hot and spicy flavour.

Purple basil: Attractive purple leaves with a nice aroma and a sweet flavour.

Radish: Green and purple leaves with white stems. Typical radish flavour.

Red garnet: Stunning reddish pink leaves and stems with a mild beetroot like flavour.

Rocket: Dark green leaves with white stems and a strong peppery flavour.

Salad burnett: Light green leaves with a aromatic melon like flavour.

Shiso: Amazing blotched purple, red and green colour leaves with a curry like flavour and hints of cinnamon.

Sorrel: Light green colour leaves with a sour flavour.

Baby leeks: are similar in size to the bottom end of spring onions. They are harvested 16-20 weeks after sowing and are milder than the older variety with a great visual appeal. They are great in stir-fries and can be used for soups, stews and even salads.

Taro: is quite easily found at the local greengrocer or supermarket and is high in thiamin, iron, vitamin B and C, niacin and fibre and several other vitamins and minerals. It has a similar shape to a sweet potato and a taste between this and a typical potato. It is light cream in colour with these amazing dark specks through it leaving a delightful decorative look. Both the tuber and the leaves are edible but taro should not be eaten raw, it must be cooked to destroy any calcium oxylate crystals that will be present. Taro can be roasted, boiled or fried and can be served as a roast vegetable or even mashed. Basically you can use it as you would a standard potato.

Crispy Skinned Salmon Fillet with Micro Herb, Fennel and Fried Taro Salad, Grilled Baby Leeks and White Wine Beurre Blanc Sauce

This is an amazing light dish perfect for summer and hot days throughout the year. The combination of flavours that are created within the salad provide a fresh finish to the strong taste of the salmon.

Serves 4

1 side of salmon with skin on (approx 1kg) trimmed and divided into 4 even pieces
20 baby leeks
1 small taro
selection of picked micro herbs
1 small fennel, trimmed and finely sliced

White wine beurre blanc sauce
100ml white wine
30ml lemon juice
100ml cream
100g diced butter

Generously and evenly salt the skin of the salmon and fry in a hot frypan. Leave for a couple of minutes being careful not to burn the skin. Flip over and grill the other side. If the salmon is thick, finish it off in the oven for 5 minutes but don't cook it past medium. It should be cooked medium-rare for the best result, anything past this will leave the salmon too dry and flavourless.

Trim the leek at both ends and fry slowly in a frypan and finish with a little butter at the last minute.

Peel the taro then peel off some thin ribbons. Deep-fry them until they go a very pale brown colour. This can also be done in a frypan with a generous amount of oil. Leave to cool on some paper towel. They will crisp up when cooled.

Carefully toss together the herbs, fennel and taro chips to make the salad.

Place the cream, wine and lemon juice into a saucepan and cook until it reduces to half of the original volume. Quickly whisk in the butter until fully incorporated and remove from heat. Add a little salt to taste.

Orange and Macadamia Nut Crusted Barramundi Fillet

The combination of macadamia nuts and oranges are an old favourite. This crust adds a fresh, sweet nutty dimension to the fish and is complimented by the lemon butter sauce which adds extra moisture with a tartish finish.

½ cup crushed macadamia nuts
¼ cup breadcrumbs
rind of 1 orange, finely grated
1 teaspoon parsley, chopped finely
1 teaspoon salt
2 tablespoon melted butter
juice of half an orange
4 barramundi fillets, skinned

Mix together the nuts, breadcrumbs, parsley and salt. Now add the butter and juice and combine well.

The mix should be able to hold together when pressed without being too wet. Press firmly onto the fish fillet and mould into a generous covering.

Pre-heat oven to 180°C. Place the fish onto a baking tray and bake for 10-15 minutes.

Serve with a nice salad and lemon butter sauce.

Lemon Butter Sauce

¼ cup white wine
1 tablespoon fresh lemon juice
1 cup cream
150g butter, diced

Place wine, lemon juice and cream in a saucepan and bring to the boil.

Reduce to a slow simmer and cook until liquid is half the original volume.

Remove from heat and whisk in the butter until well combined.

Blue Swimmer Crab Pasta with Chilli, Lemon, Garlic and Coriander

This is a popular dish using crab that is very fresh, clean and light. It is very quick to cook and looks amazing when finished.

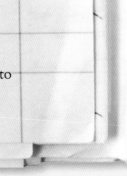

Serves 2

1 whole blue swimmer crab
2 cups cooked fettuccini
2 tablespoons chopped onion
1 teaspoon crushed garlic
1 teaspoon sliced chilli
90ml white wine
juice of half a small lemon
2 tablespoons olive oil
2 tablespoons chopped coriander

Place crab in salted boiling water for 4 minutes then cool in cold water. Clean crab and remove meat keeping the claws for decoration.

Cook fettuccini as per packet directions.

Cook onion in a frypan until soft with little colour.

Add garlic and cook for 2 more minutes.

Add chilli and again cook for a further 2 minutes being careful not to burn.

Add white wine and cook until the liquid reduces in volume by two thirds.

Add crab and toss through. Remove from heat.

If fettuccini is cold, dip into some boiling water for 1 minute then add to the crab mix.

Toss in the lemon juice and olive oil and finish with the coriander.

Paperbark Wrapped Barramundi Fillet with Slow dried Tomatoes, Roasted Red Onion, Mango and Baby Rocket

Paperbark is perfect as a wrap for meats such as fish or chicken, it also makes a great garnishing mat and will add a real outback touch to platters. The trees themselves are protected in some areas, especially in the public view because stripping the bark can leave the tree looking unsightly and reduce the trees resistance to fire and insect attack.

The bark in best kept in the fridge as it will last longer and be easier to use. All you do is just cut to size and wrap around the meat and grill on each side on a hot plate. It's great for the barbecue. The bark will infuse the meat with a mild smokey flavour while keeping it very moist by keeping in the natural juices and flavours of the meat and acting as insulation.

When serving, the bark will peel off quite easily leaving little trace that it was even there.

Alternatively, the meat can be wrapped and placed straight into the oven for 15 minutes and this will still work fine but you will find that the smokey taste will be very mild and you will get a better result by grilling it first. This works particularly well on white fish such as barramundi and can also be used on root vegetables such as sweet potato.

This is a very fresh, light and healthy dish perfect for the hot weather. It is extremely simple to make but the flavours involved are a magical combination that complement each other bite after bite. From the sweetness of the onions and mangos, to the tartness of the tomatoes, balanced so well with the mild peppery taste of the rocket.

The fish will take on a very light smokey flavour which will be well matched with the fresh salad and will tantalise every tastebud.

Serves 4

1kg barramundi fillets
1 paperbark roll

4 Roma tomatoes
salt
2 red onions
30ml olive oil
2 mangoes
wild rocket leaves

Cut the fish into 4 equal portions.

Cut the paperbark twice the size of the fish to allow enough bark to cover it.

Lightly salt the fish and wrap in the bark with the join at the bottom. The bark will stick to the fish quite well.

Grill the wrapped fish either side to start the cooking process and then place into a pre-heated 180°C oven for 10 minutes. You will need very little oil, if any, when grilling the fish.

For the salad

Cut the tomatoes into 8 pieces lengthways. Cut them into quarters and then each piece into half discarding the core. Place onto a tray and sprinkle with salt and place into the oven at 100°C for approximately 1 hour or until they have shrunk to half the size.

Peel the red onions keeping the core intact and cut lengthways into 8-12 wedges. The core will hold the wedges together. Toss in olive oil and salt, place on a tray and roast at 160°C for approximately 20 minutes or until the onions are soft without any major browning.

Slice the mango into slithers and toss together with the onions, tomatoes, olive oil, and a pinch of salt with the rocket leaves. Place this evenly on the side of four plates and then place the fish next to it. The fish can be served in the bark but it should be peeled off before eating.

Paperbark Wrapped Barramundi Fillet
with Slow dried Tomatoes, Roasted Red Onion,
Mango and Baby Rocket

Grilled Lamb with Macadamia Infused
Sweet Potato Mash, Wilted Wild Rocket,
Smoked Pear and Blue Cheese Sauce

Grilled Lamb with Sweet Potato and Macadamia Nut Mash, Wilted Wild Rocket, Smoked Pear and Blue Cheese Sauce

This dish holds an amazing combination of several ingredients creating an outstanding contrast of flavours, textures and colours.

Serves 4

Blue Cheese Sauce

½ onion, peeled and roughly chopped
2 cloves garlic, smashed, whole
2 sprigs thyme
1 small carrot, peeled and roughly chopped
600ml cream
2 bayleaves
8 peppercorns
1 tablespoon salt
30g butter
30g flour
100–150g blue cheese

Combine onion, garlic, thyme, carrot, cream, bayleaves, peppercorns and salt into a saucepan.

Bring to the boil and simmer for 5 minutes.

Remove from heat and strain, discarding the solids.

In a clean saucepan, melt butter then add flour and cook for 2 minutes stirring regularly.

Add cream, mix and bring to the boil. Simmer for 3 minutes then stir in the blue cheese.

Adjust the amount of blue cheese to taste.

Sweet Potato and Macadamia Nut Mash

500g sweet potato, peeled and roughly chopped into chunks
250g potato, peeled and roughly chopped into chunks
100g macadamia nuts
1 tablespoon butter
salt and pepper

Cook sweet potato and potato in separate pots of boiling salted water for 15-20 minutes until they show little resistance when poked with a small knife. The potato will take a little longer than the sweet potato.

Roast the macadamia nuts in the oven for 5-8 minutes until golden brown. Roughly chop.

Mash both potatoes together, add butter and salt and pepper to taste then add macadamia nuts.

Wilted Wild Rocket

2 tablespoons butter	Melt butter in a large frypan on medium heat.
400g wild rocket leaves with stems removed	Add rocket and cook for 3-4 minutes tossing regularly.
1 teaspoon of good sea salt	Add salt and toss through.

Lamb Racks

2 whole lamb racks

Clean excess meat off the bones by scraping them with a small knife.

Score diamond pattern into the fat of the lamb by cutting diagonally then turning the lamb 45°C and cut again.

Cut each rack between the bones into 2 equal portions. Sear fat-side-down in a hot pan for 3-5 minutes until golden brown.

Sear each side for 1-2 minutes to capture the natural juices and flavours and place into the oven for 10-15 minutes at 200°C.

For the best results serve medium-rare.

Smoked Pear

3 teabags
1 teaspoon brown sugar
1 pear

Remove tea from teabags and combine with brown sugar.

Cut pear into quarters. Diagonally cut out the piece of core from each quarter then cut into thirds to make a total of 12 pieces. Arrange onto a small wire rack.

Place tea and sugar mix into a large fry-pan and top with rack. Cover completely with foil. Heat pan until smoke appears and then reduce heat to supply a consistent stream of smoke for 20 minutes then remove from heat. This works well on a barbecue with a cake rack and a large metal bowl.

To assemble: Place a small dollop of sweet potato towards the edge of the plate. A nice shape can be achieved by using a small cookie cutter. Fan 3 pieces of pear next to the sweet potato towards the centre of the plate. Cut the lamb in half, weave together the bones and place next to the pear and potato. Drizzle a little of the sauce on the other side and then finally top with the wilted spinach.

Char-Grilled Moreton Bay Bugs served on Bisque-laced Gnocchi

The Moreton Bay bug is a species of slipper lobster found throughout the waters of the northern half of Australia. They live on the sea bed in deep muddy, sandy and cloudy water. They are active at night, remaining buried in sediment with only their eyes and feelers exposed during the day.

  The flesh of the Moreton Bay bug is very versatile. It can be cooked in a variety of ways such as deep-frying, boiling, grilling, steaming and stir-frying. They can also be marinated for different flavour combinations.

Serves 4

Ingredients	Method
2 raw lobster shells	Break up lobster shells and place into the oven in a large baking dish at 200°C for 10-15 minutes until bright red and brittle.
Bisque	Cook onion in a large pot with a little oil until soft with no colour.
1 onion, sliced	Add garlic and cook for another 2 minutes.
2 garlic cloves, chopped	Add lobster shells, crush and stir into the onion.
250ml cognac brandy	Cook for 3 minutes then add cognac and cook until liquid reduces to half the original volume.
1 small carrot, chopped	
1 large celery stalk, chopped	Add carrots, celery and tomato and cook for 5 minutes being careful not to burn on the bottom.
2 tomatoes, chopped	
1.5 litres water	Add water, thyme, dill stalks, saffron threads, bay leaves and peppercorns and bring to the boil. Reduce heat to a light simmer and cook for 75 minutes.
4 sprigs thyme	
6 dill stalks, leaves removed	
pinch of saffron threads	Strain through a fine sieve into another smaller pot pressing down on the solids.
2 bay leaves	
8 black peppercorns	Return to the heat and simmer until liquid has reduced to three-quarters of the original volume.
75ml cream	
75ml coconut milk	Add cream and coconut milk then simmer for 5 minutes.
3 teaspoons cornstarch	Dissolve cornstarch in the water and whisk into the bisque. Bring to the boil for another 2 minutes then remove from heat.
2 tablespoon water	

Gnocchi

500g potatoes
salt and pepper
1 egg, lightly beaten
200g plain flour

12 bugs

Peel potatoes and boil in salted water until they show little resistance when poked with a small sharp knife. Strain and let sit for 5 minutes to steam.

Mash very well to remove all lumps or force potatoes through a fine sieve, pressing down with the back of a spoon to force them through into a large mixing bowl.

Add salt and pepper and mix in the egg until well incorporated.

Mix in the flour half at a time with a wooden spoon to form a smooth dough.

You may not need to use all of the flour.

Divide the mixture into 4 pieces and roll into a log about 2.5cm wide using extra flour to dust the bench to avoid sticking.

Cut lengths of about 2.5cm and roll gently to form an oval shape. Press lightly with the back of a fork to create small ridges in the dough.

Drop each piece of dough into a pot of boiling salted water and cook until they rise to the surface. Do not over-load the pot. This should take about 2 minutes. Remove with a slotted spoon or sieve and drain well.

Place into iced water for 2 minutes if gnocchi is to be used at a later time.

To assemble: Cut the bugs in half lengthways and remove the insides leaving the meat. Place cut-side-down on the char-grill or on a hot oiled pan for 2-3 minutes then turn them over and cook for a further 1 minute.

Grill the gnocchi in a hot oiled pan until golden brown and toss through a little of the bisque and some chopped parsley.

Place gnocchi into a bowl and top with the bugs or remove the meat for easier handling.

Camel Scotch Fillet with Truffle-infused Field Mushrooms, Home-Made Potato Wedges and Red Wine Jus

Camels have been used for centuries for their meat, milk, as a form of transport, and is some countries, for their blood. A whole camel provides a substantial amount of meat with some species weighing up to 650kg. The meat tastes a lot like beef but is slightly more course and more flavoursome. It should be cooked medium-rare or medium and it will take on marinades quite well.

Truffle oil is an amazing addition to foods adding a great aroma and a tasty background flavour matching well with mushrooms, beef, potato, egg, dressings, etc. It even works well drizzled over dishes such as risotto or pasta just before serving.

Serves 4

Potato wedges

oil to fry

6 large potatoes, skin on, cut lengthways into wedges

Truffle-infused mushrooms

600ml truffle oil

6 large field mushrooms

salt to taste

Heat a pot of oil to 180°C. This can be tested by placing a cube of bread into the oil and it should turn golden brown within 10 seconds.

Cut potatoes lengthways into 6 or 8 wedges and prepare a tray lined with paper towel.

Carefully place wedges into the oil making sure not to over-load the pot as this will cool the oil down too much preventing the chips to cook properly.

Stir occasionally to prevent the chips from sticking.

Cook for 15-20 minutes until wedges are golden brown. Remove onto the tray to drain.

Make sure the oil has reached it's temperature again before doing each load.

Remove stalk from mushrooms and place onto an oven tray.

Lightly sprinkle salt over the mushrooms and drizzle with truffle oil.

Bake in the oven at 160°C for 8 minutes.

1kg camel scotch fillet
red wine jus (see page 145)

Grill the camel for 2 minutes each side in a hot pan. Finish in the oven for 10 minutes at 200 C. Let the camel rest for 5 minutes before serving.

Place on top of a nice pile of wedges and top with some sliced mushrooms. Drizzle with a generous amount of red wine jus.

Camel Scotch Fillet with Truffle-infused
Field Mushrooms, Home-Made Potato
Wedges and Red Wine Jus

Grilled Barramundi Resting on a Leek
and Potato Fondue with Gumleaf Salsa
Verde and Crisp Sweet Potato Chips

Grilled Barramundi Resting on a Leek and Potato Fondue with Gumleaf Salsa Verde and Crisp Sweet Potato Chips

Gumleaf oil is a very unique addition to your cooking. It must be used very carefully as its strength can be extremely overpowering and unpredictable. You must also make sure that you get the food grade variety as anything else may prove to be inedible. It is available online and from gourmet delis.

Gumleaf oil goes well with, and is commonly used for, a hollandaise sauce to top off steak or eggs benedict or even for some freshly cooked asparagus. It can also be used in a crème caramel, brulee or any custard based dessert. It is also commonly used with smoked salmon.

My personal favourite is to make a salsa verde, 'green sauce', and is similar to a pesto style sauce. Using it this way makes a great addition to your favourite meal and can be drizzled around the side giving the option to incorporate it into the dish without overpowering everything else. Being a green sauce it also gives the impression that it could have actually been made from the gum leaves which will be a great conversation starter at the dinner table.

This is a very simple recipe that can be modified to fit your own requirements. You can use whatever herbs you have around the garden as long as there are at least 3 types and stay away from any dominating herbs such as rosemary and thyme. The use of the gumleaf oil is to create an aftertaste and you don't want it to be the main flavour. You still want to taste the main ingredients of the dish but have a hint of the gumleaf taste.

Serves 4

Gumleaf salsa verde
½ cup parsley leaves, washed
½ cup basil leaves, washed
½ cup mint leaves, washed
½ cup coriander leaves, washed
2-4 drops of gumleaf oil
juice from ½ lemon
1 teaspoon crushed garlic
1 tablespoon Dijon mustard
½ teaspoon salt
60-80ml olive oil

Blitz all herbs in a food processor for 30 seconds then add the remaining ingredients. Add some extra olive oil if you require a more runnier sauce.

An easy way to use the gumleaf oil is to dip a toothpick in the oil then shake into the recipe.

The sauce is best made a day in advance as the flavours will incorporate better after time.

The sauce goes well with grilled fish or salmon or even lamb and beef.

Potato and leek fondue

3 potatoes
3 large leeks
1 onion, sliced
salt
½g saffron
1½ cup cream
pepper

Peel the potatoes and cut into small cubes of about 1cm squared.

Cook in salted boiling water for 5-10 minutes. Check if ready by eating a piece. Strain and rince under cold water.

Trim leeks at both ends keeping the white part. Cut in half lengthways and slice thinly on a 45° angle.

Fry onion in a large pot until soft with little colour.

Add leek and 1 tablespoon of salt and cook for about half an hour until leek becomes soft. The salt will draw out the moisture of the leek helping it to cook.

Mix saffron with 1 tablespoon of hot water and sit for 2 minutes. Now add to the leek.

Add cream and cook on a low temperature for 10 minutes.

Add the cooked potato and stir in, being careful not to break up the potato too much.

Add salt and pepper to taste.

Sweet potato chips

1 small sweet potato
olive oil for frying

Peel sweet potato into long shavings.

Heat a pot of oil to 180°C. This can be tested by placing a cube of bread into the oil and it should turn golden brown within 10 seconds.

Carefully place the sweet potato shavings into the oil without overloading as it will bubble up quite aggressively for the first couple of seconds. Cook for about 2-3 minutes without letting the chips getting too dark. Remove from oil and place onto paper towel.

The chips will crisp up while cooling and will also continue to cook for the first minute after removing so it is essential not to over-cook in the oil.

1kg barramundi fillets
olive oil

Portion the fillets into 4. Cook the barramundi by sealing both sides in a hot pan and finishing it off in the oven at 180°C for 10 minutes.

To assemble: Place a reasonable amount of the potato and leek fondue in the centre of the plate. A nice shape can be achieved by using a large cookie cutter. Drizzle a line of the salsa verde around the outside of the fondue. Carefully stack on the barramundi and then finish off by resting the potato chips on top.

Pies

It is believed that the meat pie as we know it was invented in the 1800s and was produced by combining the leftovers of roast meat and gravy within a pastry case to make it compact and portable. Originally, the pastry case was not always eaten as it was mostly tough and inedible but provided a means of transportation of the casserole-like filling. These recipes use short-crust on the pie base and puff pastry as a top.

These days there have been a lot of variations derived from the original and it is made small enough to be held in one hand. It is said that the pie should be eaten from the left hand leaving the right hand free to hold a nice cold beer. And don't forget the most important ingredient, the tomato sauce.

Traditional Meat Pie

Makes one large or 4 small pies

1 onion, diced
350g good steak, diced into 1cm chunks
600g minced beef
1 tomato, diced
1 ½ cups beef stock
3 tablespoons plain flour
2 tablespoons Worcestershire sauce
Salt and pepper to taste

Cook the onion until soft with little colour.

Add the diced steak and cook for 10 minutes until all sides start to brown.

Add mince and cook for another 10 minutes.

Add tomato and cook for a further 5 minutes.

Add flour and cook for 2 more minutes, stirring continuously.

Pour in the stock and Worcestershire sauce and cook on a low heat for 1 hour stirring occasionally.

Season to taste with the salt and pepper.

Chill then place into a prepared short-crust pastry base.

Wet edges and top with puff pastry.

Brush the top with egg yolk.

Place into a pre-heated 200°C oven for 25 minutes until pastry is golden brown.

Egg and Bacon Pie

Can be served hot or cold and makes a great breakfast.

Makes one large pie

5 eggs
3 rashers of bacon, trimmed of fat
and rind and roughly chopped
¼ cup chopped parsley
salt and pepper to taste

Pre-heat oven to 180°C. Lightly whisk eggs and add the other ingredients. Pour into a prepared short crust pastry shell.

Wet edges and top with puff pastry. Glaze the top with egg yolk and pierce with a sharp knife. Cook for 25 minutes at 180°C.

Short-Crust Pie Base
300g plain flour
125g butter, chilled and finely
chopped
1 teaspoon salt
1 egg
1 tablespoon chilled water

Process flour, butter and salt in a food processor until mixture resembles breadcrumbs.

Whisk egg and chilled water in a bowl until combined, then with food processor motor running, add to flour mixture.

Process until mixture begins to form large clumps, stopping machine before mixture forms a ball. Add more water if necessary.

Turn pastry out on to a work surface and knead gently to bring together. Wrap in plastic wrap and refrigerate for at least 2 hours.

Pre-heat oven to 180°C. To cook the base, roll out on a floured bench then place into a pie dish. Prick in several places with a knife or fork to prevent air bubbles. Top with a piece of grease-proof paper then pour in some rice or rock salt and push towards the edges. Bake in the oven for 10 minutes until golden.

Simple puff pastry
250g plain flour
salt
250g butter
squeeze of lemon juice
5-6 tablespoons iced water

Place flour and salt into a food processor, add butter and pulse 3-4 times. Don't make butter disappear, it should be lumpy.

Place in a bowl and add lemon juice and iced water. Knead to bring together but don't over-knead. Wrap in cling film and rest in fridge for 30 minutes.

Turn over, dust with flour, and roll into a rectangle 50-60cm long.

Fold ends over to make a square a third of original size. Turn 90° and roll again.

Do this three times then wrap in cling film and rest in fridge for 30 minutes.

Makes 500g or enough for two pie tops.

Mediterranean Vegetable Risotto

For this recipe, I have made the vegetable section separately as this can keep in the fridge for about 5 days or you can even keep it in the freezer for later use. This can also be added to other dishes such as a quiche or frittata or even savoury muffins or bread.

Serves 4

Vegetable mix

2 red capsicum, seeds removed
1 large zucchini
1 eggplant
1 tomato
1 red onion, peeled
4 garlic cloves
handful of mushrooms (optional)
olive oil
salt and pepper

Pre-heat oven to 180°C. Roughly dice all vegetables discarding the ends. Toss in the olive oil and salt and pepper.

Roast in separate trays on 180°C for approximately 10 minutes until soft. You still need a slight firmness.

Roughly blitz all ingredients into a food processor leaving the mix slightly chunky and not too smooth.

Refrigerate.

Risotto

2 litres boiling salted water
(or vegetable stock)
1 onion, finely diced
4 cloves garlic, crushed
500g Arborio rice
100ml white wine

It is important to have a pot of salted boiling water (or vegetable stock) on the stove when cooking the risotto so it won't slow down the cooking process.

Cook the onion on a medium heat for about 2 minutes until transparent. Add the garlic and cook for another minute until it changes to a slight brown. Add the rice and cook out for another minute until the outside of the grain starts to go transparent.

Add the white wine and let the rice absorb the liquid. Reduce heat slightly to prevent rice from sticking to the bottom. Gradually start adding the boiling water with a ladle and stir into the rice, waiting for the rice to fully absorb the water before adding any more. This should take approximately 18-20 minutes. Don't leave! Too little water and the rice will be inedible, too much water and it will be sloppy. Add a generous amount of vegetable mix to the risotto, throw in a couple of cubes of butter and finish with some parmesan cheese.

To serve, either place into a bowl and top with some shaved parmesan cheese or for a more delicate presentation you can grill some thinly sliced zucchini and wrap around the risotto and top with roasted cherry tomatoes and fried basil leaves.

Grilled Kangaroo with Beetroot Mash, Charred Artichokes, Baby Beetroot Leaves and Illawarra Plum Sauce

This dish is an amazing combination of two great Australian products. The strength of the kangaroo is enhanced by the tartness of the Illawarra plums and balanced out nicely with the sweetness of the leaves, finished with the beetroot mash.

Serves 4

600g peeled potatoes
200g peeled beetroot
salt and pepper
800g kangaroo loin
butter
6 artichoke hearts
2 handfuls of swiss chard (beetroot leaves)

Boil the potatoes and beetroot separately until they show no resistance when poked with a knife.
Mash together, season with salt and pepper and some butter.
Grill the artichokes each side until golden brown.
Grill the kangaroo for 3 minutes each side until medium-rare.

Illawarra plum sauce
½ small red onion, diced
200g Illawarra plums
70ml balsamic vinegar
70ml red wine
½ cup brown sugar
1 tablespoon honey
salt

In a stainless steel saucepan, cook the onion on low heat without producing any colour. Increase heat slightly and add the Illawarra plums, vinegar and red wine and cook until the liquid has reduced to a quarter of its original volume. Add the sugar and honey and cook slowly for a further 10 minutes. You may need to add a couple of tablespoons of water if the sauce is looking too dry. Season with the salt.

To serve: place the mash in the middle of the plate. Surround the mash with 3 artichoke halves and top with the leaves. Place the kangaroo on top and drizzle with the Illawarra plum sauce.

Aussie Outback Pizzas

Crispy Pizza Base

1 cup warm water
1½ teaspoons sugar
1½ teaspoons active dry yeast
3 cups high gluten flour
1 tablespoon vegetable oil
1 teaspoon salt

Combine water, sugar and yeast and let sit until fully dissolved.

Combine flour, oil and salt in a large bowl or mixer. It is important that you use flour with a high gluten content (12% protein or higher) in order to make the crust crispy.

Pour the yeast mixture into the flour mixture and combine until a dough forms. You may need to add a little extra water to bring it together, but not too much though.

Roll the dough into a ball and place into a large bowl. Cover the bowl with plastic wrap and let sit for 1 hour until the dough has doubled in size. For ultimate results, place into the fridge for 24 hours and then bring back to room temperature before using. This allows the yeast to work long and hard to develop the dough's texture and flavour.

Pre-heat the oven to 180°C. Now roll the dough out as thinly as possible into the desired size. I like to keep it 'out of shape' to give it that rustic look. Prick the dough with a fork at 3cm intervals to prevent large air bubbles forming.

Rub lightly with olive oil and sprinkle with good sea salt. Cook for 4-6 minutes. Cooking the base first will allow it to become crisper.

Another great touch is to quickly grill the base on a char-grill or on the barbecue to give it that smokey toasted flavour.

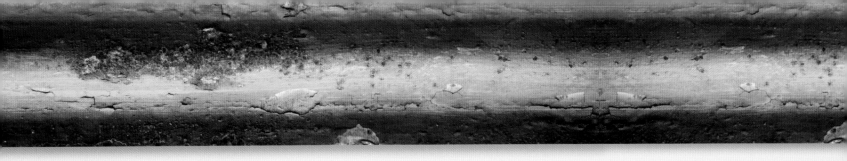

Bush Tomato Sauce

The bush tomatoes add a unique angle on the tomato base having a pungent earthy tomato flavour with a caramel-type background.

½ brown onion, roughly diced
2 cloves garlic, finely chopped
200ml white wine
4 large tomatoes, roughly chopped
75ml white vinegar
1 large sprig of thyme
2 bay leaves
3 tablespoons sugar
8 tablespoons ground bush tomato
pinch of salt and pepper

Cook onion in a saucepan on low heat with a little oil for 3-5 minutes until soft.

Add garlic and cook for a further 2 minutes stirring regularly.

Add white wine and cook until wine reduces to a third of original volume.

Add tomatoes, vinegar, sugar, thyme, bay leaves and bush tomato and cook on low heat for 15-20 minutes until it resembles a chunky sauce. Stir vigorously.

You may need to add a little water for consistency.

Add salt and pepper to taste and cool before using. Remove thyme and bay leaves.

Crocodile Pizza with Lemon Myrtle and Warrigal Greens

The amazing combination of the crocodile and the lemon myrtle is enhanced dramatically with the fresh 'spinach-like' flavour of the Warrigal greens. The croc should be sliced into strips about 2-3mm thick. Lightly sprinkle the croc with the lemon myrtle and pan fry it beforehand. This will seal of the croc and give it a slight smokey flavour from the lemon myrtle.

1 pizza base
6 tablespoons bush tomato sauce
handful of Warrigal greens,
blanched for 3 minutes
red onion, finely sliced
150g crocodile tail fillet
1 tablespoons lemon myrtle
1 teaspoon baby capers
Mozzarella cheese

Spread the pizza base with the tomato sauce.

Add a light covering of the Warrigal Greens and top with a small sprinkle of the red onion.

Prepare the crocodile and lemon myrtle as per the introduction and randomly place over the pizza.

Sprinkle the capers and top with the cheese.

Bake for 10 minutes at 200°C.

An optional drizzle of sour cream is also a great addition.

The Warrigal greens can also be replaced with spinach if desired.

Kangaroo Pizza with Mountain Pepper and Bush Tomato

This pizza incorporates several exciting ingredients from the native Australian backyard on top of a crispy thin crust. It has an amazing balance of sensations, starting off light but finishing quite substantially in an amazing combination of flavours leaving the palate demanding more.

For the pizza, a kangaroo fillet is best used. Seal the fillet all around and then cut against the grain into 5mm thin strips. This will ensure maximum tenderness for the roo.

The mountain pepper is a great alternative to typical cracked black pepper. It has a fairly intense hot pepper and chilli type flavour with an amazing fruity finish.

2 Roma tomatoes
1 pizza base
8 tablespoons bush tomato sauce
several leaves of wild rocket
red onion, thinly sliced
150g kangaroo fillet
ground mountain pepper
mozzarella cheese
blue cheese

The tomatoes are better done the day before. Remove the core and cut lengthways into eights. Sprinkle generously with salt and set aside for an hour. Now place them on a tray, discarding the liquid, and bake them at 60°C for five hours. The tomatoes will have an intense flavour and are great just to eat on their own.

Pre-heat the oven to 200°C. Spread the base with the tomato sauce then top with the rocket.

Sprinkle on a small amount of the red onion.

Prepare the kangaroo as per the introduction and place slices over the pizza. Fill the gaps with some of the dried tomatoes.

Sprinkle a little of the mountain pepper and top with the mozzarella cheese. Randomly sprinkle a small amount of the blue cheese.

Bake for 10 minutes.

Bundy and Pineapple Glazed Ham with Seeded Mustard Potatoes

This is a bumped up version of the traditional baked ham with lashings of bundy to add this amazing twist on a great dish. The ham matches extremely well with the seeded mustard cooked potatoes to finish off this substantial meal that won't sit too heavy in your stomach. An exciting dish for Christmas day or even for the Easter break.

Serves 4

Bundy and pineapple sugar syrup
½ large pineapple, peeled, cored and cut into small chunks
3 cups water
1 cup sugar
150ml Bundaberg rum
1 cup water
1kg of ham

Cook the pineapple with three cups of water. Simmer for 5-10 minutes then blitz in a food processor. Cook for another 3-5 minutes to thicken up the puree.

Add 1 cup of water, the sugar and the bundy and simmer lightly for 10 minutes until it resembles a syrup. Pre-heat the oven to 180°C.

Score the ham into diamonds and generously rub 1/4 of the syrup into the ham. Bake. Rub another quarter of the syrup into the ham every 10-15 minutes until it's all gone.

Seeded mustard potatoes
800g chat potatoes
1 tablespoon butter
1 tablespoon flour
300ml thickened cream
2 tablespoon seeded mustard

Cut the potatoes in half and cook in boiling salted water until the potatoes hold no resistance when poked with a small knife.

Melt the butter in a saucepan then add the flour. Cook for 2-3 minutes then add the cream.

Whisk until the cream comes to the boil then remove from heat. The sauce will have thickened by now.

Add the seeded mustard and a little salt then toss with the potatoes.

To serve: slice generous portions of the ham, serve with the potatoes and with your favourite vegetables. Enjoy.

Turkey Breast Rolled with Apricot, Fig and Sage Stuffing

A great dish for Christmas day. In this recipe, the fresh figs can be substituted for the dried ones and this still works quite successfully. They match well with the dried apricots and the sage adds that extra fresh boost to the stuffing leaving you with a light, fresh feeling without the bloated heavy touch.

Serves 4

1 large turkey breast
200g dried apricots, sliced
200g dried figs, thinly sliced
6 leaves of fresh sage, finely sliced
3 tablespoons balsamic vinegar
4 tablespoons brown sugar

Clean the turkey breast of any excess scraps and remove the tenderloin.

Remove all meat from the scraps and blitz with the tenderloin in a food processor.

Combine the turkey mince, sage, apricots and figs.

Lightly beat out the turkey breast until reasonably flat and approximately 1–2cm in thickness.

Place the stuffing on the breast in the middle and roll each end over.

Put onto some cling-film and roll into a log then twist the ends to tighten. Hold this together by wrapping with another piece of cling-film. The turkey can be cooked in a steamer for approximately half an hour.

It can also be wrapped in foil (still in the plastic) and cooked in the oven for approximately 1½ hours at 180°C.

Slice carefully and serve with your favourite roast vegetables and sauce.

The Great Aussie Barbecue

Nothing beats the great Aussie tradition of a barbecue on a hot day with family and friends and an esky full of ice-cold beer. It can be as simple as some chops and sausages on a slice of bread or as dramatic as marinated meats, patties, wrapped fish and salads.

Marinated skewers are a favourite for everyone. With options of diced beef, lamb, chicken, fish, shellfish or even crocodile the creations are endless. A popular one is the old prawn and pineapple, otherwise known as the 'shrimp on the barbie'. There are two reasons why you marinade your meat. The first is to add flavour, and the second is to tenderise the meat.

A simple vegetarian option is to skewer small pieces of different coloured capsicum, zucchini, red onion, squash, cherry tomatoes and brush with some pesto or even some olive oil and lemon juice.

Oriental Marinade

1 cup soy sauce 2 tablespoons fresh lime juice 3 tablespoons sesame oil 1 tablespoon sugar 1 tablespoon fresh ginger, chopped 4 cloves garlic, finely chopped ½ bunch coriander roots, finely chopped ½ cup olive oil	Combine all ingredients and marinate meat for at least 2 hours.

Yoghurt, Apricot and Mint Marinade

Great for chicken and pork.

½ cup plain yogurt 1 teaspoon crushed garlic 1½ tablespoons chopped parsley 2 tablespoons chopped mint 2 tablespoons dried apricots, finely chopped ¼ teaspoon ground ginger salt and pepper to taste	Combine all ingredients.

Honey and Clove Marinade

100ml honey
100ml white wine vinegar
5 cloves
300ml water
200ml extra virgin olive oil

Bring honey, white wine vinegar, and cloves to the boil and reduce by half. Add water and olive oil and bring to the boil then strain.

Tandoori Marinade

600ml natural yoghurt
1 tablespoon coriander powder
1 tablespoon garam marsala
1 tablespoon turmeric
20g ground ginger
juice of one lemon
1 tablespoon ground garlic

Combine all ingredients and marinate meat for at least 2 hours.

Basil Pesto Marinade

300g basil leaves
75g fresh garlic
150g shaved parmesan
100g roasted pine nuts
500ml olive oil
juice from ½ large lemon
salt and pepper to taste

Combine all ingredients in a food processor until smooth.
   Try replacing the basil with sun-dried tomatoes (oil included) for a sun-dried tomato pesto.

Sour Cream, Lemon and Mustard Marinade

¾ cup sour cream
¼ cup white wine vinegar
2 tablespoons Dijon mustard
1 tablespoon fresh lemon juice
1 teaspoon salt
½ teaspoon cracked black pepper
1 teaspoon honey

Combine all ingredients.

Simple Satay Marinade

1 cup peanut butter
1 cup coconut milk
2 tablespoons sweet chilli sauce
1 tablespoon lemon juice
1 teaspoon crushed garlic

Combine all ingredients and marinate meat for at least 2 hours.

Barbecue Marinade

100ml tomato sauce
2 tablespoons Worcestershire sauce
2 tablespoons red wine vinegar
2 tablespoons sweet chilli sauce
90g brown sugar
4 teaspoons smooth mustard
2 crushed garlic cloves
250ml water

Combine all ingredients and marinate meat for at least 2 hours.

Beer Infused Onion Rings.

To accompany meats, a guaranteed winner is some beer flavoured onion rings. Just cook some onion rings on the barbecue hotplate with a little oil and when they are half cooked, splash on a generous amount of beer and cook until ready. Great on steaks and sausages.

Grilled Potato Chips

Another winner is some homemade potato chips. Just slice some potatoes, skin-on, into round disks and toss through some olive oil, rosemary, salt and cracked black pepper. Grill on the barbecue hotplate with some extra oil.

Lemon Myrtle Smoked Fillet

A great way to impress your friends is by smoking a nice piece of fish or chicken fillet. Just place the meat on the barbecue plate and run a line of lemon myrtle next to it.

Cover with a metal bowl or a piece of foil that has been moulded into a dome shape. The lemon myrtle will begin to smoke within 30 seconds. Cook for 5 minutes then turn over the meat and cover again until cooked.

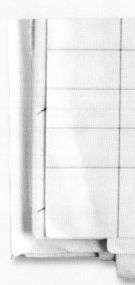

Red Wine, Rosemary and Pepper Marinated Kangaroo Fillet

This method of cooking the kangaroo will ensure maximum tenderness and great flavour and is quick in cooking making it perfect for the barbecue.

1 cup red wine
½ cup olive oil
1 large sprig rosemary
4 garlic cloves, roughly smashed but still whole
30 peppercorns (or dried pepperberries)
500g kangaroo fillet

Combine all ingredients and submerge the kangaroo in the marinade. Marinade for at least 2 hours but preferably over-night.

Slice into thin medallions and sear for 1 minute each side on a hot barbecue plate.

Banana Leaf Wrapped Whole Fish

Banana leaves are traditionally used as a wrap in Thai cooking instead of using tin foil and can be used for barbecuing, baking, or steaming foods. They not only look great, but also lend a subtle aroma and taste when foods are cooked inside them. They will also hold in the juices and flavours of the food and assist in the cooking by acting as insulation. However, some of the juices may leek during cooking so it is best to place onto a tray if cooking in the oven.

As well as cooking, they also make a pleasant background to serve various dishes on and are especially good for finger food platters. The leaf can be given a more vibrant green colour by holding it over a flame or under the grill for a few seconds.

Banana leaves store well in the fridge for up to a week or can even be wrapped in plastic wrap and placed into the freezer.

Serves 4

1 whole fish
1 lemon
¼ fennel, sliced
banana leaf
salt and pepper

Clean and gut the fish and remove scales by scraping the blade of the knife sideways across the fish from tail to head.

Cut the outside of the fish diagonally both ways, enough to go through the skin, to produce a diamond shape pattern.

Cut the lemon in half and cut two slices from the inside of each half and reserve. Squeeze the lemon halves over the outside of both sides of the fish and then chop each half into 4 pieces.

Fill the fish with the lemon and sliced fennel.

Cut the banana leaf into a rectangle approximately two and a half times the size of the fish.

Sprinkle the salt and pepper on the fish and place 2 wheels of lemon on each side.

Place the fish on the banana leaf and add some fennel leaves.

Carefully wrap the fish by folding the sides over like a parcel and fix with 2 pieces of butchers twine.

Cook on the barbecue for 10 minutes each side. The banana leaf will act like an oven, holding in the heat as well as keeping the fish moist and flavoursome.

To serve, place the fish on a plate with the fold side down. Remove the twine and cut a cross into the leaf and fold back the flaps. The aroma will be magnificent with a clean lemon smell to reveal a moist and tasty fish.

Hamburgers

One of the most popular and easy recipes for a barbecue. There are many alternatives to the meat pattie but this recipe is by far the easiest and still packs a punch with flavour. The most common mistake that people make when preparing these is not cooking the onion first, hence biting into a nice raw piece of onion half way through their pattie.

Makes 9 medium-sized burgers

1 onion, diced
2 cloves garlic, crushed
1 carrot, peeled and grated
1 tomato, seeds removed and finely diced
500g mince beef
1 egg
3 tablespoons chopped parsley
salt
cracked black pepper

Cook onion in a saucepan until it starts to turn a very light brown.

Add garlic and cook for a further 2 minutes.

Now add carrot and cook for a further 3 minutes.

Add tomato and stir for 1 more minute.

Now add this mixture to the mince and mix in well.

Thoroughly mix in egg and chopped parsley, then salt and cracked pepper to taste.

Roll into medium-sized flattened balls. This is easier with damp hands.

Cook for approximately 4 minutes each side.

These make a great meal on their own with mashed potato, vegetables and topped with gravy or are great on a piece of bread with the trusty tomato sauce.

Grilled Calamari

Grilled calamari is a great addition to your barbecue. It's really easy to prepare and very easy to cook and also extremely quick. The calamari can be infused with many flavours and it works well with a sprinkle of lemon myrtle.

To prepare the calamari, trim 2mm from each end of the tube then cut in half lengthways so as it opens up into one larger sheet. Cut fine diagonal slices on the inside of the tube about 5mm apart being careful not to go all the way through. Now do the same going the other way to produce a small diamond pattern. Cut into 4-6 manageable sized square pieces.

To cook, sprinkle finely with lemon myrtle and lay flat with the cut side down onto the hot barbecue plate and cook for 10 seconds. Turn over and hold flat with the spatula for another 10 seconds. Release spatula and the calamari will instantly curl. Serve immediately or cool down for later use in a salad. Do not over-cook the calamari as this will make it tough.

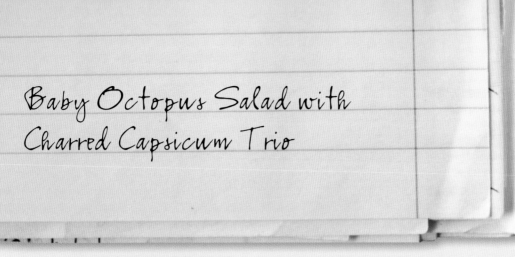

Baby Octopus Salad with Charred Capsicum Trio

1 tablespoon of sweet chilli sauce	Combine sweet chilli sauce, lemon juice and olive oil and toss with the octopus.
juice of 1 lemon	Marinate for 2 hours.
¼ cup olive oil	Drain thoroughly and cook on char-grill or hotplate for 3 minutes each side.
10 baby octopus	Do not over-cook as the octopus will turn to rubber and be inedible.
1 red capsicum	Brush the capsicums with oil and cook on each side until the flesh starts to blister and blacken.
1 green capsicum	The skin will easily peel off and wash away under cold running water to reveal a fresh, vibrant, colourful flesh.
1 yellow capsicum	Remove the insides and tear into strips then toss through the octopus.

Blue Swimmer Crab Cakes

Makes approximately 12 cakes

200g blue swimmer crab flesh
1 small chilli, finely diced
2 slices red onion, very finely diced
15 leaves coriander, chopped
½ teaspoon fish sauce
1 teaspoon sea salt
¾ cup bread crumbs
juice of half a lime

Combine all ingredients in a bowl.

Roll into mini balls about the size of a flattened golf ball.

It is easier to roll the balls if you have wet hands.

Cook for approximately 2 minutes each side. These crab cakes cook very quickly and you do not want to over-cook them as they will go like rubber bouncy-balls.

Sauces, Dressings, Chutneys and Jams

Riberry Sauce

This recipe can be served as both sweet or savoury and goes perfectly with warm puddings and fruit pies or even on ice-cream. It is also great with any game meat such as kangaroo or emu or any white meat such as chicken and is absolutely amazing with pork.

250g riberies
80ml balsamic vinegar
70ml red wine
1 cup brown sugar

In a saucepan, cook the riberries with the vinegar and red wine until the liquid has reduced to one quarter of its original volume. Add the sugar and cook slowly for a further 10 minutes. You may need to add a couple of tablespoons of water if the sauce is looking too thick.

This sauce will last for weeks in the fridge.

Fig Compote

1 cup sliced dried figs
100ml balsamic vinegar
100g firmly packed brown sugar
1 teaspoon ground cinnamon
100ml water

Bring all ingredients to the boil in a saucepan.

Reduce heat to a slow simmer and cook for 10-15 minutes until it resembles a chutney-like sauce.

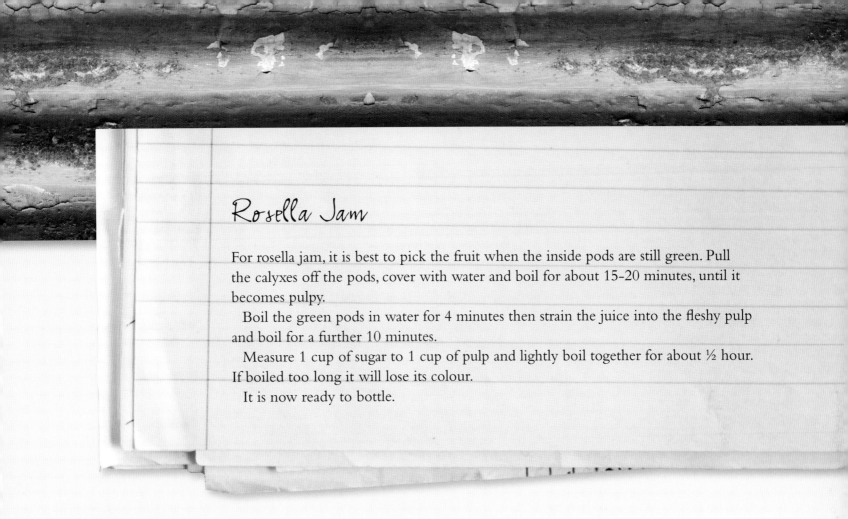

Rosella Jam

For rosella jam, it is best to pick the fruit when the inside pods are still green. Pull the calyxes off the pods, cover with water and boil for about 15-20 minutes, until it becomes pulpy.

Boil the green pods in water for 4 minutes then strain the juice into the fleshy pulp and boil for a further 10 minutes.

Measure 1 cup of sugar to 1 cup of pulp and lightly boil together for about ½ hour. If boiled too long it will lose its colour.

It is now ready to bottle.

Rosella Chutney

1 firmly pressed cup rosella flowers (calyxes)
1 small onion, finely chopped
1 large pear, peeled, cored and roughly diced
100ml white wine vinegar
200g castor sugar
100ml water
½ teaspoon ground black pepper

Finely chop the rosella flowers.
Gently cook the onion until soft with no colour.

Add pear and rosella flowers and cook for 4-5 minutes until soft.

Add sugar, vinegar, water and pepper and cook gently for 30 minutes until it thickens and resembles a chutney-like sauce.

Lemon Aspen Dressing and Marinade

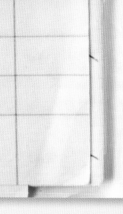

This dressing goes well with fish or even in a salad but I like it with some grilled crocodile.

Cook the lemon aspen fruit out in a saucepan with a generous amount of water. Simmer until the water has reduced to the point of sitting just above the berries then blitz them in a food processor. The puree can then be strained to remove any hard pieces of seed and then it can be frozen for later use.

The puree can also be used as a marinade for fish, shellfish or chicken. Add a little salt and oil, brush over the meat and leave refrigerated for about 2 hours. After this, wipe it off and cook as normal. You will find that the meat has taken on the lemon flavour quite well.

Dressing

1 egg yolk	Combine yolk, lemon aspen puree and mustard in a bowl.
2 tablespoons lemon aspen puree	Slowly whisk in the oil. The mixture will thicken and eventually resemble a thick dressing.
1 teaspoon Dijon mustard	
250ml extra virgin olive oil	Use in a salad or over some freshly cooked fish or crocodile.

Pepperberry Vinaigrette

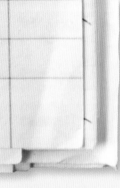

This is a great dressing that has an amazing burgundy colour and holds a distinct peppery punch with fruity undertones. It works well in salads, topped on fish or for beef and chicken dishes.

100g fresh pepperberries	Add all ingredients, except oil, to a food processor and blitz until smooth.
150ml sherry vinegar	
80g castor sugar	Slowly drizzle oil in a steady stream until well combined.
1 tablespoon Dijon mustard	Strain through a strainer.
20ml vegetable oil	

Macadamia Nut Oil

Roast 200g of macadamia nuts until golden brown. Roughly crush.

Add to 1 litre of extra virgin olive oil and heat to approximately 60°C.

Blend in a food processor and let sit until it has cooled down. Strain through a fine sieve.

The oil will take on the flavour of the nut magnificently and be a great addition to a salad or even a marinade for chicken.

Basil Oil

This oil will produce a vibrant green colour and is great for an added garnish to dishes.

Makes 250ml

boiling salted water
250g fresh basil leaves (washed)
250ml olive oil (chilled)
500ml ice cold water

Blanch quickly the basil leaves in boiling water then put them straight into the ice water.

Dry the leaves thoroughly with a cloth or paper towel.

Now place basil leaves in a deep container with the oil and blitz with a stick blender.

Let sit in the fridge for 1 hour then strain through a very fine strainer. Keep only the oil.

Keep in fridge for up to 2 weeks.

Onion Jam

1 large red onion, finely sliced 1 small baby beetroot, cut in similar strips to the onion 75ml balsamic vinegar 3 tablespoons brown sugar	Cook onion and beetroot on a low heat with a little oil until soft with no colour. Add balsamic vinegar and brown sugar and cook for 10 minutes.

Balsamic Vinaigrette

100ml balsamic vinegar 3 tablespoons brown sugar 1 tablespoon Dijon mustard 250ml olive oil	Combine vinegar, sugar and mustard in a food processor. Add oil in a slow and steady stream until combined.

Raspberry Vinaigrette

150g frozen raspberries 150ml white wine vinegar 150ml raspberry vinegar 75g castor sugar 1 tablespoon Dijon mustard 250ml vegetable oil	Bring raspberries, white wine vinegar, raspberry vinegar and sugar to the boil and slowly simmer for 5 minutes. Puree in a food processor then strain and cool and keep the solid puree. Once cool, add the vinegar mixture, the mustard and 1 tablespoon of the solid raspberry puree to a clean food processor. Add the oil in a slow and steady stream.

Basic French Dressing

3 tablespoons white wine vinegar	Combine vinegar, mustard and sugar in a bowl and whisk until well combined.
1 tablespoon Dijon mustard	
1 teaspoon caster sugar	Add oil in a slow and steady stream, whisking constantly.
¾ cup olive oil	Season with salt.

Basic Mayonnaise

This is a basic plain mayonnaise that can be flavoured with almost anything such as lemon myrtle, garlic, dill, lime juice or served plain as is. It also makes a great base to make popular dressings such as tartare sauce, cocktail sauce and Caesar dressing.

2 egg yolks	Combine yolks, mustard, vinegar and salt in a bowl.
1 tablespoon Dijon mustard	Slowly and steadily whisk in the oil. The mayonnaise will thicken quickly and can be thinned down by adding a little hot water.
1 tablespoon vinegar	
1 teaspoon salt	
200ml vegetable oil	

Tartare Sauce

250ml mayonnaise 2 tablespoons chopped gherkins 2 tablespoons chopped capers 1 tablespoon chopped parsley 2 tablespoons fresh lemon juice	Combine all ingredients well.

Caesar Dressing

250ml mayonnaise 1 small garlic clove, finely crushed 2 anchovy fillets, chopped 2 tablespoons fresh lemon juice 4 tablespoons grated Parmesan cheese	Combine all ingredients well.

Beef Stock

10kg beef stock bones
2 carrots
4 sticks celery, leaves removed
1 leek
3 brown onions
1 head of garlic
2 tomatoes
750ml of good quality red wine
6 bayleaves
10 peppercorns
6 sprigs thyme
6 parsley stems, no leaves
4 mint stems, no leaves
1 sprig rosemary

Roast bones at 200°C until dark but not burnt. Reduce oven to 150°C. Cut un-peeled carrots in half lengthways and lay cut-side-down with celery sticks onto a baking tray.

Trim leek at both ends keeping only the white and cut lengthways and lay cut-side-down onto another baking tray. Cut un-peeled onions and garlic in half horizontally and lay cut-side-down onto the same tray.

Cut tomatoes in half horizontally and lay cut-side-down on another tray and place un-peeled mushrooms on a separate tray and break apart with fingers.

Roast all vegetables at 150°C until nicely caramelised and dehydrated. The natural sugars and juices will come out of the vegetables and brown onto the tray. Do not let it go black.

Bring red wine to the boil and reduce until a quarter of the original volume.

Place all ingredients, except bones, into a large pot. Place bones on top to weigh down other ingredients.

Rub all roasting trays with some water and add to the pot making sure to get all the colour off the tray.

Fill pot with water and bring to the boil. Just before it reaches the boil, skim off anything floating on the top (oil and other impurities) using a ladle or a large spoon.

Reduce heat to a very low simmer and cook for 10 hours, skimming regularly.

Strain through fine sieve and refrigerate.

Once cooled, any remaining fat will settle on the top and can be easily removed.

Red Wine Jus

Bring the beef stock to the boil then reduce heat to a simmer.
Keep simmering until the stock reduces to one tenth of the original volume.

Chicken Stock

There are two ways of making chicken stock depending on the usage. One is white and the other is brown. The major difference is that the brown uses roasted ingredients whereas the white is made directly from the raw products.

Makes 5-6 litres

White Chicken Stock

A white chicken stock has a light clean flavour and is good for soups such as chicken and corn and also appropriate for sauces and braising liquids where little colour is required.

5kg chicken carcasses
3 celery sticks, coarsely chopped with leaves removed
1 leek coarsely chopped, discarding ends
2 large onions peeled and coarsely chopped
10 peppercorns
2 bayleaves
4 sprigs thyme
4 parsley stalks, leaves removed
2 garlic cloves

Place all ingredients into a large 10-litre pot and top with the chicken carcasses.

Fill with cold water and bring to the boil. Reduce heat to a very low simmer and skim the top regularly with a ladle or large spoon to remove any oil and impurities. Simmer gently for 6 hours

Strain through a fine sieve then refrigerate.

Brown Chicken Stock

A brown chicken stock is richer and deeper in colour and is useful where you require more flavour in sauces and soups.

5kg chicken carcasses
3 celery sticks, leaves removed
2 carrots, sliced in half horizontally
1 leek trimmed at each end and sliced in half lengthways
2 whole onions, sliced in half horizontally
1 head of garlic, sliced in half horizontally
500ml good quality white wine 10 peppercorns
2 bayleaves
4 sprigs thyme
4 parsley stalks, leaves removed

Roast bones at 180°C until golden brown in colour. Reduce oven to 150°C.

Lay celery and carrot cut-side-down onto a baking tray.

Place leek, onion and garlic cut-side-down onto a separate tray.

Roast all vegetables at 150°C until nicely caramelised and dehydrated. The natural sugars and juices will come out of the vegetables and brown onto the tray. Do not let it go black.

Bring white wine to the boil and reduce until ¼ of the original volume.

Place all ingredients, except bones, into a large pot. Place bones on top to weigh down other ingredients.

Rub all trays with some water and add to the pot making sure to get all the colour off the tray.

Fill pot with water and bring to the boil. Just before it reaches the boil, skim off anything floating on the top (oil and other impurities) using a ladle or a large spoon.

Reduce heat to a very low simmer and cook for 6 hours, skimming regularly. Strain through fine sieve and refrigerate.

Once cooled, any remaining fat will settle on the top and can be easily removed.

Fish Stock

4 large fish carcasses
200g unsalted butter
600ml dry white wine
1 onion peeled and coarsely chopped
2 celery sticks coarsely chopped
1 small carrot peeled and coarsely chopped
4 dill stalks
3 sprigs thyme
½ lemon
juice of ½ lemon
10 peppercorns
½ bulb fennel
2 bayleaves

Fry bones in a large pot with the butter.

Add white wine and cook or 5 minutes.

Add remaining ingredients then cover with water.

Bring to the boil then reduce heat to a slow simmer.

Cook for 30 minutes skimming regularly with a ladle or a large spoon.

Strain through a fine sieve then refrigerate.

Vanilla Anglaise

1 vanilla bean
1 litre milk
120g sugar
12 yolks

Split vanilla bean in half lengthways and scrape seeds into milk using the back of a knife and add the beans too. Slowly heat the milk until it reaches boiling point and then remove from heat. Sit for 10 minutes and then remove the bean.

Meanwhile, beat yolks and sugar until light.

Add warmed milk to the egg mixture then place in a heat proof bowl and stir over a pot of simmering water with a wooden spoon until thickened making sure to regularly scrape down the sides.

A good way to determine if the sauce is ready is to hold the wooden spoon vertically and run your finger through the custard. If the line runs, it's not quite ready, but if the line holds, it is.

Serve warm or chill for later use.

Wattleseed Cappuccino

The 'Wattlecino' is fast becoming popular. You can make it in a coffee machine as you would a cappuccino or latte or even by infusing some ground wattleseed with boiling water for a few minutes, strain, and then top with a dollop of whipped cream. At first, the taste seems a little different but you find yourself hooked sip after sip. And it's caffeine free.

Lemon Myrtle Hot Toddy

This is a great refreshing twist on an old Scottish favourite. The 'Hot Toddy' is great drink to sip on those colder nights before you go to bed and it is believed that it makes people feel more relaxed and less anxious. It is also believed, but not proven, that it will help fight off the flu. Make it with your favourite drop whether it be whisky or brandy.

90ml brandy
2 tablespoons ground lemon myrtle
1½ tablespoons honey
4 whole cloves
1½ cups (375ml) boiling water

Combine all ingredients well and let infuse for 3 minutes. Strain into a serving glass.

Lemon Aspen Puree

Cook the berries in a saucepan with a generous amount of water.
Simmer until the water has reduced to the point of sitting just above
the berries then blitz in a food processor. Strain.

Refreshing Lemon Aspen Beverage

In a glass, combine 2 tablespoons of lemon aspen puree with some natural
spring water for a great refreshing alternative on a hot summer's day.

Fruit Smoothies

Smoothies are a great refreshment for throughout the day or for between meals. They are very quick and extremely easy to make, not to mention they are an excellent vitamin boost and can be modified to fit in with all our dietary and health requirements. There are also many boosters available that can enhance the nutritional value turning this great tasting drink into a meal on its own.

Smoothies can be tailored to suit every need. They are low in fat and low on the calories and can be made to fit in with health requirements of lactose sensitive people, vegetarians and coeliacs. The added boosters that can be purchased range from protein enhancers, muscle builders, awakeners and added vitamins and minerals. You should carefully read about the added boosters before making a decision as many claim to work miracles when they could merely be a simple sugar additive.

As you can see, you can make a smoothie as healthy as you like by just adding natural raw ingredients. Be careful of any fruit juice that you may use as some contain sweeteners and are not as healthy as they are perceived to be. Likewise, be aware of the inferior smoothies that are available at some cafes and juice bars as a lot of frozen and processed foods may be used as well as a lot of sugar.

This recipe will give you plenty of vitamin A, B2, B3, B5, B6, B9, E, and plenty of vitamin C along with a good range of minerals and some calcium from the milk. It's great to start the day with or even for a 'pick me up' through the afternoon.

6 blocks of ice
1 small orange, peeled and diced
1 large banana, peeled and diced
1 apple, cored and diced
1 kiwi Fruit, peeled and diced
4 strawberries, top off and cut in half
1 cup skimmed milk
¼ cup natural yoghurt

Blitz the ice in a food processor until rough chunks.
Add the orange and blend for approximately 20 seconds.
Add all other fruit and blend until smooth.
Add milk and then add yoghurt.
Adjust the thickness by adding more milk or yoghurt.

But remember, it is entirely up to the individual. Sorbet or ice-cream is a good addition and even vegetable juices such as carrot, beetroot or celery.

Rosella in Champagne

Great for a special occasion or on your anniversary the rosella looks magnifient in the glass and adds a special finish to champagne.

For this beverage, the rosellas in syrup should be used from the jar. Place a single rosella flower into a champagne flute and top with a dry champagne. Adjust the flavour with some syrup from the jar.

Rosella Tea

Strip the fleshy calyx from the seed pod and discard the seeds. Place the flowers on a tray and dry in an 75°C oven for about an hour.

Place dried flowers in some boiling water and let infuse for several minutes. Try adding some honey or fresh lemon juice for a flavoursome touch. It also works well chilled.

Wattleseed Panna Cotta with Charred Pineapple

Panna cotta is a classic sweet Italian dessert. The unique flavour of the wattleseed adds a beautiful coffee and hazelnut flavour and the charred pineapple compliments this with a bitter tart taste. Also, the combination of the chilled panna cotta with the warm pineapple produces an amazing sensation in your mouth.

Ingredients	Method
2 teaspoons gelatine	Place all ingredients in a saucepan and bring to the boil.
1 ½ cups cream	Remove from heat immediately and let sit for 15 minutes.
½ cup milk	Stir then pour evenly into 4 moulds and set in fridge.
3 tablespoons sugar	Cut some small slices of pineapple and grill in a frypan until golden
1 tablespoon wattleseed	brown. Serve next to the panna cotta.

Lemon Aspen Cheesecake

This is a very simple cheesecake that is freshened up by the lemon aspen giving it a light finish with a tartish bite to an otherwise heavy dessert.

The best way to use the lemon aspen is to cook it in a saucepan with a generous amount of water. Simmer them until the water has reduced to the point of sitting just above the berries then blitz them in a food processor. The puree can then be strained to remove any hard pieces of seed and then it can be frozen for later use.

If you like, the lemon aspen can be substituted with any flavour such as a shot of espresso, mango puree, crushed tim-tams, etc. the only limit is your imagination.

250g plain sweet biscuits
120g melted butter
250g cream cheese
100g castor sugar
4 tablespoons lemon aspen puree
150ml cream (half-whipped)
1 tablespoons gelatine

Finely crush the biscuits either in a food processor or with a rolling pin in a bag or tea-towel.

Combine the crumbs with the butter and press into a cake tin or other mould to make the base.

Beat the cream cheese with the sugar then carefully add the lemon aspen mix.

Place the gelatine in approximately 3 tablespoons of warm water, stir and sit for 2 minutes. Add the gelatine to the cream cheese mixture and then add in the cream.

Beat well for 1 more minute then place into a mould and refrigerate for 3-4 hours until set.

Garnish the cheesecake with some finely grated lemon and lime rind and some of the lemon aspen berries. A nice sweet berry sauce would also be perfect.

Apple and Riberry Crumble

The addition of the riberries to this apple crumble are a true match made in heaven. They add an amazing clove-like flavour with a slight tartish hit which really balances out the sweetness of the crumble and omits the need to add cloves to the apple.

12 apples ¼ cup sugar 1 cup water 100g riberries, lightly crushed	Peel, core and chop apples into small chunks. Place into a saucepan with the sugar and water and cook on a low heat for about 30 minutes. At first the apples may look a little dry but when heated a lot of juice will come out. Add the riberries at the last minute and stir in well. Place into an oven dish.
Crumble 1 cup flour 2 tablespoons butter ½ cup dark brown sugar ½ cup rolled oats (optional)	Pre-heat the oven to 180°C. Rub flour with butter until it resembles breadcrumbs. Mix in the sugar followed by the oats. Press onto the apple and bake for 25 minutes at 180°C.

Lemon Sorbet Resting in a Rosella Cup

Sorbet serves well between courses to cleanse the palate, leaving you ready to take in the flavours of the next dish. It also makes a popular non-fat alternative to ice-cream for a refreshing dessert.

Sorbet is typically a frozen dessert made from sugar syrup and fruit puree or juice. It is a dense and flavourful product that is often infused with wine or liqueur for an extra touch.

This is a great flavoured dessert with the tartness of the sorbet balancing out the sweetness of the rosella. It also makes for a great texture combination too.

Lemon Sorbet

1 cup water
1 cup sugar
juice from 5 large lemons
zest from 2 lemons, finely grated
rosella flowers

Bring the water and sugar to the boil in a small saucepan ensuring sugar is completely dissolved.

Remove from the heat, and let cool.

Add the lemon juice and zest and pour into an ice-cream machine. Freeze according to the manufacturer's instructions.

Alternatively, if you don't have an ice-cream machine, pour mixture into a baking tray and stir the sorbet every half hour to break up the ice crystals. You may have to run it through the blender if it freezes too solid or if it separates into its components.

For this dessert it is best to use preserved rosellas in sugar syrup.

Place a generous scoop of sorbet into a rosella flower and drizzle with the syrup from the jar.

Lamingtons

The true origin of the lamington is questionable and there are several versions of how it come about. One version is that the Queensland Governor who served Queensland between 1895-1901, Baron Lamington, had come up with the idea to use up, and disguise, excess stale cake. It is also thought that this might have even been an accident by dropping the stale cake in some chocolate and then dipping it in coconut to avoid messy fingers. Ironically, Baron Lamington was believed to have hated the dessert. Other stories vary quite considerably.

One truth is that lamingtons are traditionally made using stale cake but these days, due to their popularity, they are being produced using fresh sponge. They are cut into a cube with 40mm sides and covered with thin chocolate icing and then rolled in desiccated coconut. They are quite commonly found in supermarkets, delis, coffee lounges, bakeries and lunch bars and are often filled with jam and served with whipped cream. A lemon variety has also proved to be popular.

Lamingtons have traditionally been the main ingredient behind fundraising for youth groups throughout Australia such as the Scouts and Guides. These events are called Lamington Drives and are made up of volunteers helping to make and distribute the lamingtons.

Chefs and cooks alike have tried experimenting with variations of this dessert but nothing comes close to the original.

Sponge Cake

½ cup of butter
1 cup sugar
2 eggs
1 ½ cups self-rising flour
½ cup of milk

Pre-heat oven to 180°C. Beat butter and sugar until light and fluffy.

Add eggs one at a time and beat well.

Add flour and milk folding in carefully and alternating as you go.

Pour into a greased or lined rectangular cake tin and bake at 180°C for 30-40 minutes. Allow to stand for 5 minutes then turn out onto a cooling rack to cool.

Icing Mixture

4 cups icing sugar
1/3 cup cocoa powder
½ cup milk
2 tablespoons butter
2 - 3 cups desiccated coconut

Cool the cake for at least half an hour in the freezer, then cut into squares. It may be easier to leave in the freezer overnight.

Combine the sugar and cocoa in a large bowl.

Heat the milk and butter in a saucepan until the butter is melted.

Add the milk mixture to the cocoa mixture and mix to a fluid yet not runny consistency.

Using a fork, roll sponge squares into icing then into the coconut and place onto a cooling rack to set.

Once they have dried, place in an airtight container and let sit for a few hours before eating.

If you like, cut the squares in half and spread with a thin layer of jam then join back together before icing.

Anzac Biscuits

The acronym ANZAC was born in 1915 when Australian and New Zealand soldiers were training in Egypt and has become associated with their landing at Gallipoli on 25 April 1915.

The ANZAC biscuit come about during the first world war due to the soldiers families concern with the condition and nutrition of food that was being supplied to them. The food was carried on slow travelling ships with limited refrigeration facilities for up to 2 months. Because of this, the families come up with a biscuit that contained ingredients that didn't readily spoil. The main difference is that the biscuits did not contain eggs and were bound together using golden syrup or treacle.

These days ANZAC biscuits are still a popular choice and are found on supermarket shelves all across the country. They also provide an easy recipe that is made quite regularly in the family kitchen. Around ANZAC Day, these biscuits are also often used by veterans' organisations to raise funds for the care of aged war veterans.

1 cup rolled oats
1 cup plain flour, sifted
1 cup caster sugar
1 cup desiccated coconut
125g butter, chopped
1 tablespoon golden syrup
2 tablespoons boiling water
1 teaspoon bi-carbonate of soda

Preheat oven to 160°C.

Combine oats, flour, sugar and coconut.

In a small saucepan, combine butter and golden syrup on a low heat until melted.

Combine water and bi-carb soda and pour into butter mixture.

Combine the dry mixture with the wet mixture.

Roll small balls about the size of a golf ball and arrange onto a greased tray leaving approximately a 4cm space in between each one. Press lightly to flatten.

Bake for 15-20 minutes or until golden brown.

Stand for 5 minutes before transferring them to a wire rack to cool.

Makes approximately 35 biscuits.

Pavlova

The Pavlova is a meringue type dessert that is crispy on the outside but light and fluffy on the inside. It is traditionally served with lashings of whipped cream and multiple pieces of mixed fresh fruit with sweet and tart flavours such as strawberries, kiwi fruit, passionfruit, banana and berries. It is frequently eaten during holiday periods such as Christmas.

There has long been a debate between Australia and New Zealand about the true origin of this famous dessert but it is believed that it was created in Perth in 1935 to celebrate the visit of a great Russian ballerina, Anna Pavlova.

2 egg whites
1½ cups castor sugar
½ teaspoon vanilla
1 teaspoon vinegar
1 teaspoon cornflour
4 tablespoons boiling water

Place all ingredients into a clean dry bowl and beat with an electric mixer on high until mixture is stiff and sugar has completely dissolved, approximately 15 minutes.

Line an oven tray with foil. Brush with melted butter and dust with cornflour, shaking off the excess.

Spread onto the prepared tray. This will make one 28cm pavlova or you can make several smaller ones.

Pre-heat oven to 180°C. For an electric oven: bake at 180°C for 10 minutes then reduce heat to 140°C and bake for a further 45 minutes. Cool in oven. If making smaller ones, reduce the cooking time at 140°C.

For a gas oven: Bake at 180°C for 10 minutes then reduce heat to 140°C and bake for a further 1 hour. Cool in the oven.

Do not open oven during cooking process. When cooked turn oven off and leave pavlova in oven until it has cooled down. It is also safe to leave in the oven overnight ready to decorate the next morning.

Macadamia Nut, White Chocolate and Malibu Cake

200g butter	Pre-heat oven to 180°C or 160°C for fan-forced ovens.
1½ cups sugar	Cream butter and sugar until light.
3 eggs	Add eggs one at a time beating well.
1 cup (200g) white chocolate buds	Add white chocolate and macadamias and fold in flour and milk to make a smooth batter.
1 cup (150g) chopped roasted macadamias	Pour mixture into a 25cm lined and greased cake tin.
1¾ cups self-raising flour	Bake for approximately 1 hour.
1 cup milk	Poke with a wooden skewer and it should come out clean.
	Cool on a wire cake rack.

Malibu Ganache

A general guideline for making ganache is 1 part cream to 3 parts chocolate.

1 cup white chocolate	Bring the cream and Malibu to the boil in a saucepan.
¼ cup cream	Remove from heat and stir in the chocolate until fully combined.
2 shots (60ml) of Malibu	Let sit to cool down then spread over the cake.
	Garnish with some melted white chocolate drizzled over the top.

Wattleseed Chocolate Mousse

The combination of chocolate and wattleseed is a true match made in heaven. The addition of the wattleseed in this mousse gives it an amazing background flavour. Try substituting the hot water for a shot of good espresso for that extra kick.

2 tablespoons wattleseed
1 tablespoon hot water
250g chocolate
4 eggs separated at room temperature.
1 tablespoon castor sugar
250ml cream (whipped)

Combine wattleseed and hot water and let sit to infuse for 5 minutes.
   Place chocolate in a heatproof bowl over a pot of gently boiling water and stir until melted.
   Beat egg whites to a soft peak then beat in sugar until combined.
   Carefully fold whites into chocolate mixture by adding a little at a time.
   Carefully fold in the cream.
   Refrigerate for 2 hours.
   Top with whipped cream and a sprinkle of wattleseed.
   Makes 6-8 serves.

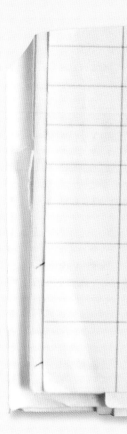

Lavender Brulee

Lavender is one of those flowers that we think of more as a perfume or room freshener rather than an ingredient that we cook with. For this reason, a lot of us will tend to steer away from trying this unusual plant but lavender has been used in traditional English and European cooking for centuries.

There are many varieties of lavender and they all vary in fragrance. You should select the sweeter scented variety for cooking and while both the stems and flower can be used, the flower will provide a better flavour. Choose only EDIBLE lavender.

Lavender goes well with meat such as lamb, chicken, pork and even game meats and it is quite often used in custard-based desserts and works very well with chocolate. Care must be taken when using lavender as it can prove to be quite over-powering. It has a flavour much like how it smells only a milder taste with a slight citrus undertone and an amazing floral background.

500ml milk
8 buds fresh lavender
6 egg yolks
50g sugar

Bring milk and lavender buds to the boil then remove from heat. Let sit for 10 minutes.

Whisk the egg yolks with the sugar until it thickens and lightens in colour.

Remove buds from milk and stir the milk into the egg mixture with a spoon, do not whisk. It's alright if some leaves have stayed in the milk.

Pour into moulds and place these into a dish with about 2cm of water on the bottom.

Place carefully into a pre-heated oven at 130°C for approximately 1 hour.

Brulees will be ready when you tap the sides and it holds like a jelly. There should be no liquid.

Remove from water and let brulees sit for 30 minutes.

They can be chilled if desired.

To finish the top, sprinkle lightly with castor sugar and use a small blow torch to caramelise the sugar. You can also heat up an old spoon in a gas flame until really hot then run smoothly over the sugar.

Pancakes

Pancakes are very easy to prepare and even easier to cook and are great for breakfast or even lunch and can be served in a hundred different ways. They can be made sweet or savoury and topped with almost anything. Maple syrup is a very popular choice with lots of fresh fruit as is a nice chocolate or caramel sauce or even a big scoop of ice-cream. You could even try mixing the batter with savoury ingredients such as smoked salmon or cracked pepper.

½ cup plain flour	Combine dry ingredients then add egg and enough milk to make a batter. The thinner the mixture, the thinner the pancake will be.
½ cup self-raising flour	
2 tablespoons of sugar	Pour a small amount of the pancake mixture into a hot oiled pan.
1 egg	Flip once when bubbles start to appear evenly across the surface.
1½ cups milk	Serve immediately.

Weights and measures

Volume and weight are two different forms of measurements. We can't assume that 1 cup of something is going to weigh 250g. The weight of an ingredient can vary because several different things such as the density of the product, the humidity in the air, how well it is packed in the cup etc. When measuring dry or solid ingredients, dip the cup or spoon measure into the food and lift out. Use the edge of a knife to scrape across the surface, removing excess ingredients so the surface is flat. When measuring liquids, place the jug onto a flat surface and check at eye level as it will appear different from standing above it.

Here is an approximate guideline for commonly used ingredients.

Cup conversions for metric & imperial measurements

ingredient	1 cup		1/2 cup		1/3 cup		1/4 cup	
breadcrumbs, dry	90g	2¾oz	45g	1½oz	30g	1oz	25g	¾oz
butter	250g	8oz	125g	4oz	80g	2 ½oz	60g	2oz
cheese, shredded/grated	80g	2 ½oz	40g	1oz	35g	1oz	25g	¾oz
choc bits	190g	6oz	95g	3oz	70g	2¼oz	55g	1¾oz
coconut, desiccated	85g	2¾oz	45g	1½oz	35g	1oz	20g	½oz
flour, plain/self-raising	150g	4¾4oz	75g	2½oz	50g	1½oz	40g	1½oz
rice, uncooked	200g	6½oz	100g	3oz	70g	2¼oz	50g	1½oz
sugar, brown – lightly packed	160g	5oz	80g	2½oz	60g	2oz	45g	1½oz
sugar, brown – firmly packed	200g	6 ½oz	100g	3oz	70g	2¼oz	55g	1¾oz
sugar, caster	220g	7oz	115g	3¾oz	80g	2½oz	60g	2oz
sugar, icing	150g	4¾oz	80g	2½oz	60g	2oz	45g	1½oz

Metric cup & spoon sizes

Cup	Metric
1/4 cup	60ml
1/3 cup	80ml
1/2 cup	125ml
1 cup	250ml
Spoon	**Metric**
1/4 teaspoon	1.25ml
1/2 teaspoon	2.5ml
1 teaspoon	5ml
2 teaspoons	10ml
1 tablespoon (equal to 4 teaspoons)	20ml

Liquids

Metric	Cup	Imperial
30ml		1 fl oz
60ml	¼ cup	2 fl oz
80ml		3 ½ fl oz
100ml	$^1/_3$ cup	2 ¾ fl oz
125ml	½ cup	4 fl oz
150ml		5 fl oz
180ml	¾ cup	6 fl oz
200ml		7 fl oz
250ml	1 cup	8 3/4 fl oz
310ml	1¼ cups	10½ fl oz
375ml	1½ cups	13 fl oz
430ml	1¾ cups	15 fl oz
475ml		16 fl oz
500ml	2 cups	17 fl oz
625ml	2½ cups	21½ fl oz
750ml	3 cups	26 fl oz
1L	4 cups	35 fl oz

Mass / weight	
10g	1/4oz
15g	1/2oz
30g	1oz
60g	2oz
90g	3oz
125g	4oz (1/4 lb)
155g	5oz
185g	6oz
220g	7oz
250g	8oz (1/2 lb)
280g	9oz
315g	10oz
345g	11oz
375g	12oz (3/4 lb)
410g	13oz
440g	14oz
470g	15oz
500g (1/2 kg)	16oz (1lb)
750g	24oz (1 1/2 lb)
1kg	32oz (2lb)

Temperature

Celsius (electric)	Fahrenheit	Gas mark	
120°	250°	1	very slow
150°	300°	2	slow
160°	325°	3	moderately slow
180°	350°	4	moderate
190°	375°	5	moderately hot
200°	400°	6	hot
230°	450°	7	very hot
250°	500°	9	very hot

If using a fan-forced oven, the golden rule is to turn it down 20°C and the cooking time may also be a little quicker. For example, if a recipe calls for a cake to be baked at 180°C, turn the oven down to 160°C.

Index